# ADOBE CREATIVE SUITE 6
## Introduction to InDesign, Photoshop & Illustrator

STEP BY STEP
TRAINING

noble desktop

Adobe | AUTHORIZED
Training Center

Published by:
**Noble Desktop LLC**
594 Broadway, Suite 1202
New York, NY 10012
www.nobledesktop.com

This book was typeset using Linotype Syntax Pro and printed and bound in the United States of America.

## FINAL PROJECT

## REFERENCE MATERIAL

**Thank you for purchasing a Noble Desktop Course Workbook!**

These instructions tell you how to install the class files used in this workbook. There are two ways to get the files: from the included CD, or downloading them from our website. The CD and download contain the same files, so use whichever method is more convenient.

### ( INSTALLING CLASS FILES FROM THE CD )

**Never open files directly from the CD — always copy the folders to your hard drive or you may get unexpected results!**

1. Navigate to the **Desktop**.

2. Create a **new folder** called **Class Files**.

3. Put the Class Files CD in your computer.

4. Open the CD, but **do not open any individual folders.**

5. Select all of the folders if there is more than one.

6. Drag them all into the **Class Files** folder you just made.
   These are the files you will use while going through the workbook.

7. Eject the CD.

   That's it! Enjoy.

### ( DOWNLOADING & INSTALLING CLASS FILES )

1. Navigate to the **Desktop**.

2. Create a **new folder** called **Class Files** (this is where you'll put the files after they have been downloaded).

3. Go to **nobledesktop.com/download**

4. Enter the code **adobe-cs6-1302-01**

5. If you haven't already, click **Start Download.**

6. After the **.zip** file has finished downloading, be sure to unzip the file if it hasn't been done for you. You should end up with a folder that has three folders inside: **Illustrator Class, InDesign Class** and **Photoshop Class.**

7. Drag those three folders into the **Class Files** folder you just made.
   These are the files you will use while going through the workbook.

8. If you still have the downloaded .zip file you can delete that.

   That's it! Enjoy.

### LETTER CREATION

*Setting Preferences*
*The Control Panel*
*Text Frames*
*Basic Text Attributes*
*Basic Keyboard Shortcuts*

### MORE TEXT STYLING

*Baseline Shift*
*Small Caps*
*Line Tool*
*Making Proper Fractions*

### ADVANCED WORD PROCESSING/FORMATTING

*Paragraph Spacing*
*Tabs*

### KERNING/TRACKING

*Optical vs. Metric Kerning*
*Kerning vs. Tracking*
*Manual Kerning*

*Continued…*

INDESIGN

**EXERCISE PREVIEW**

Scott Carson
594 Broadway, Room 1202
New York, NY 10012

June 5, 1991

Fred Smith
VP, Advertising
The Clapper
1800 Fifth Avenue
New York, NY 10101

Dear Mr. Smith:

The Clapper is wonderful! I haven't used a real light switch in months! May you live a long and happy life.

Sincerely,

Scott Carson

**EXERCISE OVERVIEW**

A basic letter—this is about as simple as it gets! This exercise will introduce you to the basics of creating a document, drawing text boxes, and formatting text.

## SETTING INDESIGN'S DEFAULT MEASUREMENTS

1. If you have any documents open, close them all.

   NOTE: By setting preferences when no documents are open you are setting the default for how new documents from now on will be created. (If a document were open you'd only be changing **that** document's preferences instead of setting the defaults as we are about to do now.)

2. (**MAC**): Go into the **InDesign** menu and choose **Preferences > Units & Increments**.
   (**WINDOWS**): Go into the **Edit** menu and choose **Preferences > Units & Increments**.

3. On the right, both **Horizontal** and **Vertical** Ruler Units should be **Inches**. If they are not, change them both to **Inches** now.

4. Now that the Preferences have been set, click **OK** to begin the first exercise.

   NOTE: Eventually, we will prefer to work in Picas. But for now, all our measurements will be in inches.

## CREATING THE LETTER

1. From the **File** menu, select **New** then **Document** and set the following:

   – Number of Pages: **1**
   – **UNcheck** both **Facing Pages** and **Primary Text Frame.**
   – From the **Page Size** menu choose **Letter.**
     (This makes an 8.5 in by 11 in page.)
   – Click the **Portrait** ( ▣ ) button to make it an upright page.
   – Set **Columns** to **1** and don't worry about the Gutter.
   – Make all Margins **1 in**

   Click **OK.**

2. Choose the **Type** ( T ) tool. When creating a text frame it may be a little hard to figure out where the active part of the type cursor is. As shown below, it's near the middle where the cross hair is.

3. Click and drag to create a text frame for the letter, using the margin guides to make sure the text frame fills the whole area inside the guides.

4. The cursor should now be blinking in the text frame. If not, click back in it.

5. From the **File** menu, select **Place.**

6. Navigate to the **Desktop,** then go into the **Class Files** folder, then into the **InDesign Class** folder. Select the text file named **LetterText.txt.**

7. From the **View** menu, select **Zoom In.**

8. Scroll so you can see the top right-hand corner of the page.

   HINT: An alternative to using scrollbars is to use the **Hand** ( ✋ ) tool. To use the Hand tool via a keystroke, hold **Option–Spacebar** (MAC) or **Alt–Spacebar** (WINDOWS). Just be sure to hold **Option/Alt** first, before pressing **Spacebar.**

9. Choose the **Rectangle Frame** ( ⊠ ) tool.

10. Create a small frame in the upper right-hand corner of the page (about **3 in** x **2 in**).

11. Make sure the frame is still selected and from the **File** menu, select **Place.**

12. Select **LetterAddress.txt.**

13. With the frame still selected, choose the **Selection** ( ▶ ) tool.

14. Hold **Shift** and click on the body text frame, now both frames should be selected.

15. Select the **Type** ( T ) tool.

16. The **Control** panel that is docked to the top of the screen should be showing the type options shown on the next page. If this panel isn't open, go into **Window > Control.**

It has two sets of options, **Character** ( A ) and **Paragraph** ( ¶ ). The two buttons on the left switch between them. If you have a smaller screen InDesign will only be able to display one section at a time. But if you have a wide enough screen InDesign will displ ay some of the other section's options in whatever space it has to the right.

CHARACTER A SECTION SELECTED

——— CHARACTER OPTIONS ———

EXTRA SPACE SHOWS
PARAGRAPH OPTIONS

PARAGRAPH ¶ SECTION SELECTED

——— PARAGRAPH OPTIONS ———

EXTRA SPACE SHOWS
CHARACTER OPTIONS

**17.** As shown below, in the **Control** panel set the following:
   • Font: **Myriad Pro Regular**
   • Font Size ( 𝐓 ): **14 pt**

---

( **NAVIGATING THE DOCUMENT—ZOOMING AND SCROLLING** )

**1.** Let's get a better feel for moving around within InDesign. We want to see the text larger on screen. Select the **Zoom** ( 🔍 ) tool.

**2.** Click a few times on the text. With each click it will appear larger.

**3.** To zoom out, hold **Option** (MAC) or **Alt** (WINDOWS) and click a few times.

**4.** Let go of the keys. Let's zoom in a different way. This time click and drag over an area you want to enlarge on the screen. When you let go of the mouse, that area will fill the entire window.

**5.** Make sure the **Type** ( T. ) tool is selected.

**6.** Click on one of the text boxes as though you are ready to edit the text.

**7.** To scroll around hold **Option–Spacebar** (MAC) or **Alt–Spacebar** (WINDOWS) and drag anywhere on the document (be sure to hold **Option/Alt** first; see sidebar for details).

   When done let go of the mouse and the keys.

**8.** To zoom back out and see the entire page, go to **View > Fit Page in Window** (or hit **Command–0(zero)** (MAC)) or **Control–0(zero)** (WINDOWS).

**9.** Instead of using the **Zoom** ( 🔍 ) tool we can use keystrokes:

   (MAC): **Command–plus(+)** to zoom in and **Command–minus(-)** to zoom out

   (WINDOWS): **Control–plus(+)** to zoom in and **Control–minus(-)** to zoom out

**SCROLLING BEST PRACTICES**

You may notice that sometimes you can scroll by using just **Spacebar** or **Option/Alt**. Since it depends on which tool you're using, we teach you to always use **Option/Alt, then Spacebar** so that you don't make unexpected duplicates of objects, or add unwanted space characters to your text.

*Letter Creation* **ADOBE CS6: INDESIGN**

## SAVING AND PRINTING (OPTIONAL)

1. Add a text frame somewhere and put your name in it so you'll know which letter is yours if you print.

2. From the **File** menu, select **Save As.**

3. Name it **yourname-Letter1,** and before clicking **Save:**

    (MAC): If you are already in the **InDesign Class** folder just click **Save.** If not, navigate to the **Desktop,** then **Class Files,** then into the **InDesign Class** folder and click **Save.**

    (WINDOWS): At the top next to **Save in,** if it already says **InDesign Class,** just click **Save.** If not, from that menu choose **Desktop.** Then go into the **Class Files** folder, and then into the **InDesign Class** folder and click **Save.**

    NOTE: Your document will be saved as **yourname-Letter1.indd** because it is an **InD**esign **D**ocument.

4. If you wish, print the letter **(File > Print).**

5. If this was super-easy for you, go to the next exercise, otherwise finish this exercise.

## MORE PRACTICE

1. Create a second letter. Follow the same steps above to create your boxes. But in the second letter, you will:
    • Place the text **ReturnLetterText.txt** and **ReturnLetterAddress.txt.**
    • Make the font of the text in this letter **14 pt Chaparral Pro Regular.**

2. Create a third letter but this time:
    • Use the text **ThirdLetterText.txt**
    • Use the same **LetterAddress.txt** from the first letter.
    • Make the font for this letter **Myriad Pro Regular.**

---

### CREATING TEXT FRAMES (WHICH TOOL TO USE)

You may wonder why we used the **Rectangle Frame** ( ⊠ ) tool instead of the **Type** ( T ) tool to create the text frame for the address. That's because we already had a text frame under the place where we wanted to create a new text frame. If we had clicked there with the Type tool we'd have started editing the text in the frame that was already there. By making a Rectangular frame first, we don't have to worry about accidentally editing the text underneath.

TIP: How can you tell if you can use the Type tool to create a new text frame? When you see your cursor with a box around ( ⛶ ) it means you can create a new text frame. When it's just the I-beam ( ⌶ ) you'd be editing text in the frame underneath the cursor and you need to use the **Rectangle Frame** ( ⊠ ) tool.

ADOBE CREATIVE SUITE 6

**EXERCISE PREVIEW**

**EXERCISE OVERVIEW**

This exercise gets you pointed in the right direction, showing you strokes, caps, how to make proper fractions, and other professional typesetting techniques.

1. From the **InDesign Class** folder open the file **uninspirationPoster.indd.**

   If you get a message about modified links, click **Update Links.** The exercise file was created on a different computer and since the images are in the same folder, InDesign will just find and update them for you.

2. We've already typed in the text and done some basic styling such as font and size. You will perfect the layout. Zoom in on the text so you can see it better.

**STYLING THE "EXPLORATION" TITLE**

1. Select the word **exploration.**

2. In the **Control** panel click the **All Caps** ( **TT** ) button.
   Don't see it? Switch to the **Character** ( A ) options via the button on the left.

3. That looks better, but we can make the Exploration title more interesting. Select the middle letters **XPLORATIO** (everything except the **E** and **N**).

4. Make those middle letters (XPLORATIO) smaller, **70 pts.**

**5.** With them still selected, let's Baseline Shift them to align with the top of the **E** and **N**. The fastest way is to use the following keystrokes:

(MAC): **Option–Shift–up** or **down arrow**
(WINDOWS): **Alt–Shift–up** or **down arrow**

Try it. Hit the keyboard shortcut until the text lines up at the top.

NOTE: To see how much your Baseline Shift is (or if you don't like keystrokes) look in the **Control** panel. You'll probably need to be viewing **Character** ( A ) options, then **Baseline Shift** ( A↑ ) is near the middle of the panel.

**6.** To fill out that space we just created we'll add a line. Select the **Line** ( / ) tool.

**7.** Hold **Shift** (to make sure the line is perfectly horizontal) and draw a line that aligns with the bottom of the **E** and **N** and fills in that space.

NOTE: The line should already be the right color (orange) as we chose that ahead of time for you. If you needed to apply a color yourself you would open the Swatches panel **(Window > Color > Swatches)** and click on the color to apply it.

**8.** With the line still selected, as shown below, in the **Control** panel make the Stroke weight **3 pt.**

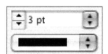

---

**STYLING THE TWO LINE SUBTITLE**

**1.** Using the **Type** ( T ) tool, select the two lines of text under **Exploration.**

**2.** In the **Control** panel click the **Small Caps** ( Tr ) button.
If you don't see it, switch to the **Character** ( A ) options via the button on the left.

---

**THE DISCLAIMER**

**1.** We need to add a footnote number to line 2 of the subtitle. Put the cursor at the end of the second line, after **"...Wrong Way."**

**2.** Type in a **1** (that's a number one).

**3.** Select the **1** and in the **Control** panel click the **Superscript** ( T¹ ) button.

**4.** Type another **1** at the beginning of the disclaimer text at the bottom of the page, which starts **"Not responsible..."**

**5.** Select it and make it **Superscript** ( T¹ ) as well.

---

**MAKING PROPER FRACTIONS**

**1.** In the middle of that line is a fraction that isn't properly styled. Select the **99/100.**

2. On the far right of the **Control** panel go into the **panel menu** (  ) and select **OpenType > Fractions.** (Refer to the bottom of the page for an alternative method.)

3. Since you'll continue to work with this file in a later exercise, be sure to save it as **yourname-uninspirationPoster** into the **InDesign Class** folder.

NOTE: To apply options such as **All Caps, Superscript,** etc. an alternative way is using the **Character panel (Type > Character)** and going to its menu ( ▾☰ ) (their keystrokes are also shown here).

---

### PROPER FRACTIONS WITHOUT OPENTYPE

While OpenType fraction styling is ideal, it won't work with TrueType or Postscript fonts. It also won't work with all OpenType fonts! If the menu has square brackets around the [Fractions] option, that particular font lacks the special fraction characters. So one of our instructors, Dan Rodney, wrote a script that formats fractions regardless of font. He's included the script for free in our **InDesign Class** folder (which is on the CD) or it can be downloaded from **danrodney.com**

**TO USE THE SCRIPT:**

1. Select the fraction you want to format.

2. Go to **Window > Utilities > Scripts.**

3. In the **Scripts** panel, open the **User** folder. If you see **ProperFraction 2.0-Size DanRodney.js** double-click it. If it's not there, you must install it using the directions below.

**TO INSTALL THE SCRIPT:**

4. Minimize or Hide InDesign so you can see the **Desktop.**

5. Go into the **Class Files** folder, then into **InDesign Class > Scripts - Mac and PC > ProperFraction2.0.**

6. Select **ProperFraction 2.0-Size DanRodney.js** and hit **Cmd-C** (MAC) or **Ctrl-C** (WINDOWS) to copy it.

7. In the **Scripts Panel (Window > Utilities > Scripts)** you'll see **Application** and **User** folders. Scripts can be installed into either, but only admins can install into the **Application** folder. If you're not an admin, choose the **User** folder. With one of the folders selected, **at the top right** of the panel go into the menu ( ▾☰ ) and choose **Reveal in Finder** (MAC) or **Reveal in Explorer** (WINDOWS).

8. You should now see a **Scripts Panel** folder. Double-click the folder to open it, then hit **Cmd-V** (MAC) or **Ctrl-V** (WINDOWS) to paste the file.

NOTE: Dan Rodney has a Pro version of this script that will find all fractions in a document and format them. It is available for purchase at **danrodney.com**

---

## EXERCISE PREVIEW

## EXERCISE OVERVIEW

Here you will learn the basics of page layout along with more advanced text manipulation. You will utilize paragraph space before/after, leading, and tabs to complete the layout.

### CREATING THE LETTER

1. If you haven't already, we highly suggest setting InDesign's workspace to waste less space and show some more useful panels. To do this go to **Window > Workspace > [Advanced].**

2. Workspaces remember how they were last setup. To make sure we are using the default workspace, go to **Window > Workspace > Reset Advanced.**

3. **Mac** only: Since we are not using the **Application Frame**, the **Application Bar** at the top of the screen wastes space. To hide it choose **Window > Application Bar.**

4. From the **File** menu, select **New** then **Document.**

   – UNcheck **Facing Pages** and **Primary Text Frame.**
   – Choose a **Letter** page with **Portrait** ( ⬚ ) orientation (8.5 in wide by 11 in high).
   – Make columns **1.**
   – Make all margins **1 in.**

   Click **OK.**

5. (MAC): Go into the **InDesign** menu and choose **Preferences > Units & Increments.**
   (WINDOWS): Go into the **Edit** menu and choose **Preferences > Units & Increments.**

6. Change both **Horizontal** and **Vertical** to **Picas.** Click **OK.**

   NOTE: Picas are the default unit of measurement in InDesign, and are the preferred unit of measurement when styling text. For a full explanation of Picas, check out the Picas Explained page in the Reference section at the back of this book.

7. Select the **Type** ( T. ) tool and create a text frame that fills the margin guides.

8. With the cursor still in the frame, go to **File > Place.**

9. From the **InDesign Class** folder select **NewLetterText.txt.**

10. Select the **Rectangle Frame** ( ⊠ ) tool.

11. Create a small frame in the upper right-hand corner of the page (about 2 in x 1 in, or 12p x 6p).

12. Make sure the frame is still selected and go to **File > Place.**

13. Select **NewLetterAddress.txt.**

### FORMATTING THE TEXT

1. In the **View** menu, select **Zoom In** to see things larger, if necessary.

2. To view the hidden characters choose **Type > Show Hidden Characters.**

3. Select the **Type** ( T. ) tool (so the **Control** panel is showing type options).

4. With the **address** frame still selected, in the **Control** panel enter these specs:

   Font: **Minion Pro Regular**
   Size ( T ): **13 pt**

5. With the **Selection** ( ▲ ) tool, select the **body** text frame, then in the **Control** panel enter the following specs:

   Font: **Minion Pro Regular**
   Size ( T ): **12 pt**
   Leading ( A ): **13 pt**

6. With the **Type** ( T. ) tool, click in the one-line paragraph immediately under the date ("Lenny Bo Benny").

7. In the **Control** panel (at the top of the screen) on the far left side click the **Paragraph** ( ¶ ) **Formatting Controls** button.

8. In the **Control** panel, go to **Space Before** ( 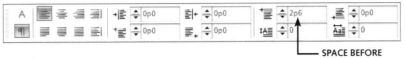 ) and enter **2p6** (refer to the screenshot below if you can't find this option).

SPACE BEFORE

9. Click in the one-line paragraph "Dear Lenny."

10. In the **Control** panel go to the **Space Before** ( ) and enter **2p6**.

11. Select the first two large paragraphs of the letter.

12. Make the **Space Before** ( ) **0p6**.

13. Select the first line of the table ("Color, etc.") and make the
    **Space Before** ( ) **0p8**.

14. Select the last paragraph of text ("Well, that's about") and the paragraph
    "Sincerely." and make the **Space Before** ( ) **0p6**.

15. Select the last line ("Henny Benny") and make the **Space Before** ( ) **2p6**.

### FORMATTING THE STATISTICS

1. Highlight the entire first line of the statistics (Color...).

2. In the **Control** panel change the font to **Minion Pro Bold.** Don't see this option?
   Switch to the **Character** ( A ) options via the button on the left.

   TIP: To choose the bold version of the current font hit **Command–Shift–B** (MAC)
   or **Control–Shift–B** (WINDOWS).

3. Click in the second line of the statistics (Blue...).

4. In the **Control** panel's **Paragraph** ( ¶ ) options under **Space Before** ( ),
   enter **0p3**.

5. Highlight every line of the statistics including the category line.

6. In the **Control** panel's **Character** ( A ) options make the Leading ( ) **12 pt.**

### TABS

1. With all lines of statistics still highlighted, go to the **Type** menu and choose **Tabs**.

2. At the top left of the **Tabs** panel that appears, click the **Left-Justified Tab** ( ↓ )
   button if it isn't already chosen.

3. As shown below, add a tab by clicking in the small white space above the small tab ruler—the small arrow ( ↓ ) shows you where it has been placed.

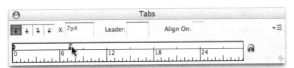

4. Drag the arrow ( ↓ ) until **10p** shows up in the **X** field.

5. Click again on the small ruler near the **18p** mark.

6. Drag the new arrow until **18p** shows up in the **X** field.

7. Add one last tab at **26p**.

8. If everything looks good, close the **Tabs** panel. If not, adjust the tab arrows ( ↓ ) to their proper position, then close the panel.

### ( WRAPPING THINGS UP )

1. Make sure the Rulers are visible. If they are not go to **View > Show Rulers.**

2. Choose the **Selection** ( ▶ ) tool.

3. Click on the body text frame.

4. Grab the **top middle handle** and drag the top of the box **down** to about **12p** on the left ruler.

5. Add a text frame somewhere and put your name in it so you'll know which letter is yours if you print.

6. From the **File** menu, select **Save As.**

7. Name the document **yourname-BigLetter,** and then choose where to save the file:

> (MAC): If you are already in the **InDesign Class** folder just click **Save.** If not, navigate to the **Desktop,** then **Class Files,** then into the **InDesign Class** folder and click **Save.**

> (WINDOWS): At the top next to **Save in,** if it already says **InDesign Class,** just click **Save.** If not, from that menu choose **Desktop.** Then go into the **Class Files** folder, and then into the **InDesign Class** folder and click **Save.**

8. Print the letter if you wish.

**EXERCISE PREVIEW**

Before — Notice the sloppy, large spacing between
the letters, especially between the "O" and the "N".

After — A tighter, more even spacing helps
give the heading a polished professional look.

### EXERCISE OVERVIEW

Proper kerning and tracking are some of the finer elements of a well typeset design.
Here you will track and kern the headlines to give the title a finished look.

1. Open the file **yourname-uninspirationPoster.indd.** If you didn't get a chance
   to complete the exercise earlier in class open **uninspirationPoster-Done.indd**

2. Zoom in a lot on the text so you can see it well.

3. Look at the space between the letters. Look for letters that have gaps between
   them or are too close together, possibly touching. For instance, the **O** and the **R**
   in **Exploration** are quite far apart; in the two line subtitle the word **Way** appears
   several times. There is too much space between the **W** and **a**.

### OPTICAL VS. METRIC KERNING

Every font has built-in kerning called **metrics.** But not all fonts do a good job
of kerning, and what if you have one letter of one font, and another letter
of another font? InDesign can do kerning for you based on the shape of the
characters. InDesign calls this Optical kerning.

1. Use the **Selection** ( ![cursor] ) tool to select the **Exploration** text frame.

2. Switch to the **Type** ( T ) tool so the **Control** panel displays the text options.

3. Near the middle of the **Control** panel's **Character** ( A ) options you'll see
   the **Kerning** ( AV ) option. From the **Kerning** ( AV ) **pop-up** ( ⊕ ) menu
   choose **Optical.**

   While it's not quite perfect, it's definitely better.

4. Use the **Selection** ( ![cursor] ) tool to select the two line subtitle below.

5. Switch to the **Type** ( T ) tool and again choose the **Optical** kerning.

6. In this case the kerning is worse! The gap next to the Ws is bigger. Optical is not always better. It all depends on the font and the particular letters used. Switch back to **Metrics** for this two line subtitle.

### ( MANUAL KERNING )

1. Regardless of whether you're using Optical or Metric kerning you might not be satisfied with the result so you can manually kern what you don't like. You'll mostly use keystrokes to adjust the amount of kerning, but InDesign's default amount for these shortcuts is a bit big. In the **InDesign** menu (MAC) or **Edit** menu (WINDOWS), choose **Preferences** and then **Units & Increments.**

2. Set **Kerning/Tracking** to **5** and click **OK.**

   NOTE for former Quark users: **5** in InDesign equals **1** in Quark. So a kerning of **1, 2, 3** in Quark is **5, 10, 15** in InDesign.

3. Look through both the two line subtitle and the Exploration title for bad kerning. Put the cursor between any two letters and use the following keystrokes to decrease or increase any undesirable spacing. Don't bother with the disclaimer text at the bottom. It's too small for people to really notice.

   **To kern in small increments:**

   (MAC): **Option–left arrow** (decreases space) or **Option–right arrow** (increases space)

   (WINDOWS): **Alt–left arrow** (decreases space) or **Alt–right arrow** (increases space)

   **To kern in larger increments:**

   (MAC): **Cmd–Opt–left arrow** (decreases space) or **Cmd–Opt–right arrow** (increases space)

   (WINDOWS): **Ctrl–Alt–left arrow** (decreases space) or **Ctrl–Alt–right arrow** (increases space)

   TIP: Remember that **kerning** is meant only to fix bad pairs of letters. If it's an overall, more equal correction you want then select all the text and **track** it. The same keystrokes work, but **tracking** removes/adds an even amount of space across all the **selected letters,** whereas kerning adjusts only the space between two letters.

4. When done, you'll probably need to use the **Selection** ( ▶ ) tool to adjust the width of the rule under Exploration.

5. Save the document as **yourname-uninspirationPoster.indd.**

6. If you wish, print the page, look at kerning, make any adjustments that seem necessary, then print again.

**EXERCISE PREVIEW**

**EXERCISE OVERVIEW**

Two-page spreads can be a little tricky to create, but we make it easy for you in this exercise. We'll cover facing pages and page numbering issues to show you how to do it right.

⸺ **SETTING THE DOCUMENT UP AS A 2–PAGE SPREAD** ⸺

1. From the **File** menu, choose **New > Document** and set:
   – Number of Pages: **2**
   – Start Page #: **2**
   – Leave **Facing Pages** checked
   – Leave **Primary Text Frame** UNchecked
   – Make the width **8 in** and height **10.75 in**
   – Columns **1** (don't worry about the gutter)
   – All Margins **0** (make sure the **link** (  ) button is checked on, and enter **0**)
   – Bleed **0.125 in** all around (if you don't see **Bleed and Slug,** click **More Options**)

   Click **OK.**

2. In the **InDesign** menu ⬭MAC⬭ or **Edit** menu ⬭WINDOWS⬭, choose **Preferences** and then **Units & Increments.**

3. On the right set the Ruler Units to:
   Origin: **Page** ◄— DON'T forget this option!!!
   Horizontal: **Picas**
   Vertical: **Picas**

4. Open the **Pages** panel **(Window > Pages).**

5. The pages should look like a spread as shown to the right, with a black line in the middle, separating the left and right pages. If they are not a spread, you didn't check Facing Pages when creating the document, or you didn't enter 2 as the Start Page #. To fix it go into **File > Document Setup**, check **Facing Pages**, and enter **2** as the **Start Page #.** Then click **OK.**

NOTE: The reason this worked is because even numbered pages are always on the left and odd pages on the right. Starting with CS5, InDesign now lets you specify the page number of your first page, making it easy to start with a left-hand (even numbered) page! Previous versions of InDesign always started a document with page 1 (which is a right-hand page). This made creating two-page spreads trickier. Refer to the sidebar on the right for instructions on how to do this with CS4 and older.

### BRINGING IN THE PICTURE

1. Go into **File > Place**.

2. From **InDesign Class** folder, select **time.tif** and click **Open.**

3. The cursor should now be a loaded image icon ( ) with a preview of the photo.

   Position the top left of this cursor at the **red bleed guide** (which is ⅛ **in** off the top left of the page) and click **once** to place the image.

### MAKING THE "MINI" TIME MAGAZINE COVER

We are going to put a box around the jeep and put some type in it to make it look like a mini Time magazine cover so your eye is drawn to the action.

1. Choose the **Rectangle** ( ) tool.

2. On the right-hand page draw a box around the jeep that is shaped somewhat like a magazine cover (with the jeep near the bottom). Don't worry about being too exact. Next we'll type in the exact measurements to perfect it.

3. In the **Control** panel, make sure the **top left** reference point ( ) is chosen, then enter the 4 values shown (X/Y and W/H):

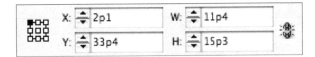

| X: | 2p1 | W: | 11p4 |
|----|-----|----|------|
| Y: | 33p4 | H: | 15p3 |

   When done hit **Return** (MAC) or **Enter** (WINDOWS) to kick in the change.

4. We want the frame to be a specific color, but before we make the color let's make sure the stroke color is active. Open the **Swatches** panel. If it's not already open, go into **Window > Color > Swatches.**

---

**SPREADS IN OLDER VERSIONS**

1. **Double-click** on **page 1** to make sure it's selected.

2. Go into the **Pages panel menu** ( ) and choose **Numbering & Section Options.**

3. Check **Start Numbering Page at** and next to it type in **2**. Click **OK.**

4. Now the first page is on the left, because even numbered pages are always on the left. The second page automatically slid up on the right, and you have your spread!

---

PAGES
[None]
A-Master
A    A
2-3
2 Pages in 1 Spread

5. As shown below, at the top left of the **Swatches** panel make sure the **stroke** swatch is in front (active). If it's not, click it to make it active.

6. Now we can create the color. From the **Swatches panel menu** ( 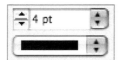 ) at the top right, choose **New Color Swatch.**

   Leave **Name with Color Value** checked and set the following:
   
           Color Type: **Process**
          Color Mode: **CMYK**
      Make the color: **0% Cyan, 100% Magenta, 100% Yellow, 0% Black**

   Click **OK.**
   Although it's hard to see, the stroke is already colored with that swatch!

7. Let's make the line thicker. As shown below, in the **Control** panel make the Stroke weight **4 pt.**

8. Let's put some type into this box. With the **Type** ( T, ) tool click in the frame and type in **TIME** (in all caps!).

9. Select that text and make it **44 pt Adobe Caslon Pro Regular.** (Note: this font is listed under **C.**)

10. As shown below, at the top left of the **Swatches** panel make sure the type's **fill** swatch is in front (active). If it's not, click it to make it active.

CLICK HERE ➔ 

11. In the **Swatches** panel click the red color you just created (it's named C=0 M=100 Y=100 K=0). That's how you color type.

12. Ooops. Let's center the text (**Align Center** ( ☰ ) button in the **Control** panel).

13. The type is too close to the top of the frame, so go into **Object > Text Frame Options.**

14. UNcheck the **link** ( ▓ ) button and make the **Inset Spacing, Top: p4.**

   Click **OK.**

## ( SETTING THE TAG LINE )

**1.** For the type below the image, create a text frame in the white area at the bottom of the **right** page, making sure the frame sits entirely on the right page—no part of the frame should fall onto the left page!

**2.** Choose the **Selection** ( ) tool and enter the following specs. (Be sure to click the **top left** reference point ( ) in the **Control** panel):

X: **2p1**      W: **28p6**
Y: **52p1**      H: **11p8**

**3.** Type in the following three lines of text:

**If you think watching a volcano in a movie is frightening,**
(press **Shift–Return** (MAC) or **Shift–Enter** (WINDOWS))

**imagine watching one in a rearview mirror.**
(press **Return** (MAC) or **Enter** (WINDOWS))

**The world's most interesting magazine.**

**4.** Select the top two lines of type. Make them **14/20 Minion Pro Regular.**

**5.** Select the next line. Make it **11/20 Myriad Pro Bold Condensed**. But also set the **Space Before** ( ) to **3p** (that's in the Paragraph panel).

## ( PRINTING AS A SPREAD )

**1.** Looks like you did it! Well, one last thing. We want to set this up to print as a spread. To do this, go into **File > Print,** but don't hit Print till we say! Here you specify a few things:

   – Choose the appropriate printer at the top.
   – Check the option for **Spreads.**
   – On the left click on the **Setup** section and set:
        Paper Size: **Letter**
        Orientation: **Landscape** ( )
        Check on: **Scale to Fit**

**2.** Now that everything's set, you can hit the **Print** button.

### EXERCISE PREVIEW

### EXERCISE OVERVIEW

This exercise shows you the often misunderstood but immensely important baseline grid. We'll also show you some new text wrap options.

### GETTING STARTED

1. Create a new document:
   – a **Letter** sized **Portrait** ( 📄 ) page
   – **UN**check **Facing Pages** and **Primary Text Frame**
   – **3** columns with a **1p6** (or 0.25 in) gutter
   – margins of Top: **12p11,** Bottom: **18p7,** Left and Right: **4p6** (make sure the link ( 🔗 ) button is checked off)
   – bleed of **p9** (or 0.125 in)

2. In the **InDesign** menu ⟨MAC⟩ or **Edit** menu ⟨WINDOWS⟩, go to **Preferences > Units & Increments.**

3. Set the **Horizontal** and **Vertical** ruler units to **Picas.**

4. Go to **Type > Show Hidden Characters** to view hidden characters.

5. Go to **File > Save As** and name it **yourname-eco-ad.indd.**

## PLACING THE BACKGROUND PICTURE

1. Draw a **Rectangle Frame** ( ⊠ ) that fills the **Bleed** guides (red guides outside the borders of your page).

2. Go to **File > Place** and select **green-grass.tif.**

3. Go to **Object > Fitting > Fill Frame Proportionally.**

4. Use the **Selection** ( ▶ ) tool and the **content grabber circle** in the center of the image to move the photo up until the tallest blades of grass just reach the bottom of the margin guides.

## IMPORTING THE TEXT

1. Make sure the **Rulers** are visible **(View > Show Rulers).**

2. Create a text frame that fills the two right column guides.

3. Switch to the **Selection** ( ▶ ) tool and keep the frame selected.

4. Go to **Object > Text Frame Options** and under **Columns** set:
   Number: **2**
   Gutter: **1p6**

5. Click **OK.**

6. Using the margin and column guides, draw another text frame that fills the first column.

7. Into the right frame, place the file **eco.txt.**

8. In the left text box, type **It's Easy Being Green.**

9. **Select all (Cmd–A MAC or Ctrl–A WINDOWS) the text.**

10. Give the text in the left box these attributes:
    Font: **Myriad Pro Bold**
    Size ( T ): **66 pt**
    Leading ( A ): **54 pt**
    Paragraph Alignment: **Align Right**

11. You will need to make the text box wider to accommodate the text. Extend the left side of the box out past the left margin guide, only enough to fit one word per line.

12. In the layout, highlight the word **Green.**

13. **Open** the **Swatches** panel **(Window > Color > Swatches).**

14. At the bottom of the palette, **Option–click** MAC or **Alt–click** WINDOWS the **New Swatch** icon and set the following:

> Color Type: **Process**
> Color Mode: **CMYK**
> Color: **C=0 M=68 Y=85 K=0**

Uncheck **Name with Color Value** and make the Swatch Name **Orange**.

15. Click **OK**. You will see the word Green gets the new orange color.

16. Give the body text these attributes (put the cursor in the text and press **Cmd–A** MAC or **Ctrl–A** WINDOWS· to select it all):

> Font: **Myriad Pro Regular**
> Size ( T̄T ): **8**
> Leading ( A̱ ): **13.5 pt**
> First Line Left Indent ( ⁺≣ ): **1p3**
> Color: **[Paper] (white)**

### CREATING THE DROP CAP AND OTHER TYPE CHANGES

1. Click anywhere in the first paragraph of the body text.

2. Make sure the **Control** panel is showing the **Paragraph** ( ¶ ) options and set:
First Line Left Indent ( ⁺≣ ): **0p**
Drop Cap Num. of Lines ( ꜟ⋏≣ ): **3**

3. The **R** of the first paragraph looks too close to the text next to it, insert the text cursor just to the right of it (between the **R and e**) and kern out ( A̱V̱ ) until it looks right.

4. Make it:
   - **Myriad Pro Light**
   - **Orange** (apply the swatch you created earlier)

5. Highlight the line/paragraph **Reduce Your Carbon Footprint.** Remove the First Line Left Indent ( ⁺≣ ).

6. Make it:

   - **Arial Bold**
   - Size: **10.5**
   - Leading: **12 pt**
   - Make the color **black**
   - Add **1p1.5** Space Before ( ⁺≣ ) the paragraph
   - Put a new **soft return** (**Shift–return** MAC or **Shift–enter** WINDOWS) just before the word **Carbon** to bump it to a new line.

7. Highlight the last two words in the right text box, **Get Involved.**

8. Make them:
   - Type style: **Bold**
   - Color: **Orange**

### SETTING THE BASELINE GRID

Look closely at the alignment of the lines of text in both columns at the bottom of the page. They don't line up any more since we changed the leading of the carbon footprint subhead. Let's fix it so both columns align again.

1. In the **InDesign** menu (MAC) or **Edit** menu (WINDOWS), go to **Preferences > Grids.**

2. Under **Baseline Grid** set the following:
   Start: **2p9**
   Relative To: **Top of Page**
   Increment Every: **13.5 pt** (This is the same as the text's leading.)

3. Click **OK.**

4. With the grid set up, we must tell the text to use it. **Select all** the text.

5. Make sure the **Control** panel is showing **Paragraph** ( ¶ ) options.

6. Click the **Align To Baseline Grid** ( ≣ ) button (located to the right of the **Hyphenate** checkbox). The lines in both columns should align again.

7. Click anywhere in the **REDUCE YOUR CARBON FOOTPRINT** paragraph.

8. Click the **Do Not Align to Baseline Grid** ( ≣ ) button.

9. Add a bit more space before the carbon footprint paragraph so it is now **1p3.**

### PLACING THE LIGHT BULB PICTURE

1. Draw a **Rectangle Frame** ( ⊠ ) in the top right corner of the page.

2. Switch to the **Selection** tool and keep the frame selected.

3. Click the **top left** reference point ( ▦ ) in the **Control** panel and set the following:
   X: **41p1**      W: **11p8**
   Y: **1p2**       H: **25p2**

4. Go to **File > Place** and select **spiral.tif.**

5. Go to **Object > Fitting > Fit Content Proportionally.**

6. Open the **Text Wrap** panel **(Window > Text Wrap)** and set the options as shown.

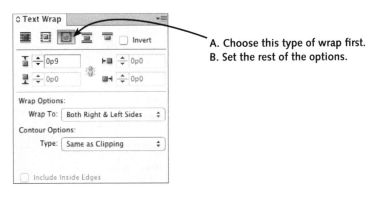

A. Choose this type of wrap first.
B. Set the rest of the options.

### "MASSAGING" THE TEXT TO FIT

We want all of the text to be visible at the bottom of the ad and both columns to be the same length. The last words should be "Get Involved." Notice that the **text overflow ( ⊞ )** symbol is showing. This means you are missing text. We'll use tracking to squeeze the rest of the text in.

1. To see how much text is missing select the **Type** tool ( T. ) and click anywhere in the text frame so the blinking cursor is somewhere in the text.

2. Go to the **Info** panel **(Window > Info).** There is a count of the **text you see** plus (+) the **overset text** (text you don't see). It should say something like Words: 350 + 11 and Paragraphs 6 + 1. This means there is one extra paragraph of 11 words overflowing. (These numbers may be different for you depending on how much kerning you applied after the Drop Cap R earlier.)

3. Go into the **InDesign** menu (MAC) or **Edit** menu (WINDOWS), choose **Preferences > Units & Increments** and set **Kerning** to **5.**

4. Select the paragraph right next to the light bulb that starts with **Making homes...**

5. Track it in using **Opt–left arrow** (MAC) or **Alt–left arrow** (WINDOWS). You can do this keystroke up to 3 times (for a value of –15) but anything more will look bad. This should track the letters in just enough to shorten the paragraph by one line.

6. Select the last paragraph of text by clicking 4 times in it quickly. Track the text in until you see the words **Get Involved.**

7. Use the **Selection** ( ↖ ) tool (while holding Shift) to move the left text box up until the top of the letter **s** in the word **It's** aligns with the top of the body text.

## ADDING THE COLOR BAR

1.  Draw a **Rectangle Frame** that fills the width between the left and right **Bleed** guides. Make it **3p3** in height. Its top should meet the top bleed guide.

2.  Open the Swatches panel **(Window > Color > Swatches)**.

3.  As shown below, at the top left of the **Swatches** panel make sure the **fill** swatch is in front (active). If it's not, click it to make it active.

CLICK HERE ➜

4.  Select **Orange** swatch.

5.  With the rectangle still selected, go to **Object > Arrange > Send Backward**. The color bar should now be behind the light bulb but above the background image.

## ADDING THE STATISTIC

1.  Draw a **Text Frame** in the top left corner of the page, about 6p (one square inch).

2.  Switch to the **Selection** tool and keep the frame selected.

3.  Click the **top left** reference point ( ▦ ) in the **Control** panel and set the following:

    X: **4p6**   W: **13p**
    Y: **3p8**   H: **7p5**

4.  Place the file **stat.txt**.

5.  Make it:
    *   **Arial Bold**
    *   Size: **12**
    *   Leading: **15 pt**
    *   **Align Right**
    *   **White**

6.  Choose the **Pen** tool.

7.  As shown below, draw an arcing **Bezier Curve** from just beside the statistic to the left edge of the light bulb.

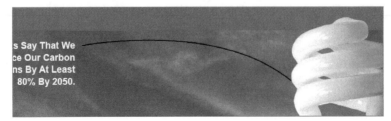

8.  Open the **Swatches** panel **(Window > Color > Swatches)**.

9. Make sure the stroke swatch is in front ( 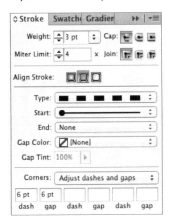 ). If it's not, click it to make it active.

10. With the stroke still selected, go to the **Swatches panel menu** ( ) and choose **New Color Swatch.**

11. Set the following: **C=50 M=0 Y=100 K=0,** and name the new swatch **Green.**

12. Once you click **OK,** the stroke gets the green swatch.

13. Open the **Stroke** panel **(Window > Stroke)** and set the options as shown.

14. Make a new text box on the clipboard, outside the page, measuring **W: 7p, H: 8p2.** Type an **asterisk.**

15. Make it:
    • **Myriad Pro Semibold**
    • **130 pt**
    • **Green** (use the swatch you created)

16. Use the **Selection Tool** and select the box.

17. Go to **Type > Create Outlines.**

18. Move the asterisk shape to the opposite end of the curve, near the light bulb.

( **FINISHING UP** )

1. **Deselect** everything, then hit **W** on the keyboard to see the lovely advertisement without guides.

2. **Save** the document and print if you wish.

**EXERCISE PREVIEW**

**EXERCISE OVERVIEW**

How did we get the head in front of the logo? In this exercise we'll show you
that trick, as well as the **Type on a Path** tool.

( **CREATING THE DOCUMENT** )

**1.** Create a new document:
   – UNcheck both **Facing Pages** and **Primary Text Frame**
   – **10 in** wide by **12 in** high
   – Margins of **0**
   – If you don't see a **Bleed** option click the **More Options** button on the right.
     Then to the right of **Bleed** make sure the **link** ( 🔗 ) button is checked on and
     in any of the four boxes enter **1/8 in.**

**2.** In the **InDesign** menu (MAC) or **Edit** menu (WINDOWS), go to **Preferences > Units &
Increments** and change the ruler units to **Picas**.

**7A**
EXERCISE

## IMPORTING THE GRAPHICS AND TEXT

We have a couple images and a text file we'd like to import. We can do this all in one shot.

1. Go to **File > Place (Cmd–D** MAC **or Ctrl–D** WINDOWS **).**

2. Navigate into the **InDesign Class** folder, then into **Interview Magazine** folder and do NOT click Open until we say!

   • Click once on **charlize.tif** to highlight it.
   • Hold **Shift** and click on **Magazine.txt.**
     This should highlight all 3 files: **charlize.tif, InterviewLogo.eps** and **Magazine.txt.**
   • Click **Open.**

3. A thumbnail image of Charlize should currently be loaded in the cursor. It should have a number (3) since this image and 2 other files are loaded in the cursor. If the cursor is showing a different thumbnail, use the **arrow keys** on your keyboard to cycle through the loaded images until Charlize shows up.

   As shown here:
   • Position the cursor at the **top left bleed guide.**
   • Click **once** to place the Charlize image.

4. The image should fill out the red bleed guides and the cursor should now be loaded with the **Interview logo.**

5. Position the cursor near the top left of the page and click once to place the logo. Do not worry about the exact placement for right now.

6. The cursor should now be loaded with some text. Drag out a text frame to the left of Charlize, on the mountains just below the sky. Refer to the exercise preview as needed.

7. With the text frame still selected, choose the **Type** ( T ) tool and make the font **Myriad Pro Bold Condensed.**

8. To refine the position of everything choose the **Selection** ( ↖ ) tool and:
   • Make the text frame start **1p2** from the left of the page and make it about **16p** wide.
   • If needed, move things around until it looks like the sample.

## STYLING THE TYPE

You will now select various lines of text and set size/leading values.
Remember that when we say 14/16, that means **14 pt** Size, **16 pt** Leading!

1. Apply these specs to the appropriate text:

Charlize — ⎤
Theron — ⎦ **62/49**

She Ain't the — ⎤
Girl Next Door — ⎦ **24/24**

Photos by Herb Ritts    **17/19**

Big, Bad    **35/45**

Brad Pitt    **46/40**

Pix!    **79/63**

Why Millions Wish — ⎤
He Were the — ⎥ **24/24**
Boy Next Door — ⎦

Clip 'n' Save!    **21/21** [Make font **Brush Script Std**]

by Steven Klein    **17/19**

2. Draw a small text frame under the **"ew"** of the Interview logo. This is for the date of the issue.

3. Type the following into that text frame: **Novembrrrr 2012**

4. Change it to **14 pt Myriad Pro Bold Condensed.**

## ( COLORING THE TYPE )

1. Make sure nothing is selected in the document by choosing **Edit > Deselect All.**

2. It's time to create some colors for the text, but first let's get rid of InDesign's default colors that we won't be using. Open the **Swatches** panel.

   We have the standard InDesign colors such as a cyan, magenta, etc., but we also have Pantone 200 CVC. How did that get there? When we imported the Interview logo, it brought with it the spot color Pantone 200 CVC. Wow, what will they think of next?

3. Go into the **Swatches panel menu** ( ▾☰ ) and choose **Select All Unused.**

4. Click the **Delete ( 🗑 )** button at the bottom of the panel.

5. We need to create two colors. Go into the **Swatches panel menu** ( ▾☰ ) and choose **New Color Swatch.** Set the following but DON'T click OK until we say!

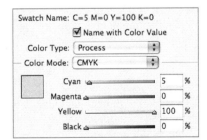

6.  Once you've entered the above color, click **Add** once (not OK!). This way you are still in the New Color Swatch window and we can make the second color.

7.  Mix up the following color and then click **OK.**

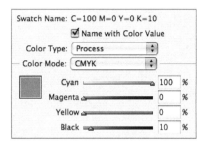

8.  We'll start by making all the text on the left white (the color of the paper we're printing on). Select the text.

9.  As shown below, at the top left of the **Swatches** panel make sure the type's **fill** swatch is in front (active). If it's not, click it to make it active.

CLICK HERE ⟶

10. In the **Swatches** panel click the **[Paper]** swatch to apply it.

11. Now we'll add dollops of color by selecting some text and choosing the appropriate swatch in the **Swatches** panel. Select the text **Charlize Theron.**

12. Click on the **yellow** swatch named (C=5 M=0 Y=100 K=0). The text color might look weird, but when you deselect it will be yellow.

13. Make the following words the same **yellow** swatch:
    Herb Ritts, Big Bad Brad Pitt Pix, Clip 'n' Save, and the "by" on the bottom line.

14. See that **Novembrrrr 2012** in the upper right of the page? Make that **Pantone 200 CVC.**

15. Select only the **brrrr** and make it the **blue** swatch named (C=100 M=0 Y=0 K=10). Lookin' good!

( **BRINGING CHARLIZE'S HEAD IN FRONT OF THE LOGO** )

Notice that the Interview logo is covering Charlize's head. This is simply unacceptable! We need to bring in another file, in which the background has been removed leaving only Charlize's forehead and hair, so that we can place it in front of the logo without the background showing up. Thankfully, this has already been done in Photoshop, which is the best place to do it. All you must do is import the silhouette and place it just right. It's easy if you follow these steps.

1.  With the **Selection** ( ▶ ) tool, click on the Charlize picture frame to select it.

2.  **Copy** it **(Edit > Copy).**

3. Go to **Edit > Paste in Place.**

4. The type and logo will look like they've disappeared, but don't worry. We've just made a second picture frame in front of everything, so it's only temporarily covering over the type and logo.

5. Now we can replace the Charlize picture by importing a silhouetted Charlize forehead into this latest frame. With the frame still selected, go to **File > Place** and choose **charlize silo.psd.**

   NOTE: Because the forehead frame is now on top of everything, you won't be able to select the text, logo, etc. for later changes. For instance, if you need to change the text, hold **Command** (MAC) or **Control** (WINDOWS) and click on it. Wow, you reached right through that top frame! With the text frame still selected go to **Object > Arrange > Bring to Front** so you won't have to keep using the keystroke to select it each time.

### THE FINAL TOUCHES

This cover is almost ready. However, let's add the word **Introducing** above the words **Charlize Theron.** In a twist, let's make it flowing type on a path. We'll try to draw a Bezier line riding the mountain range as shown in our example on the right.

1. Do an **Edit > Deselect All.**

2. Let's make sure we have a stroke color, but no fill. Near the bottom of the toolbox, below the Fill/Stroke swatches, click the **Default Fill & Stroke** ( ) button.

3. Select the **Pen** ( ) tool.

4. This can be tricky, but we'll do our best. To get the curve we are looking for, you need to create 3 anchor points, dragging to the right every time, but sometimes up, sometimes down. Below you see what the path should look like. If you have trouble, ask the instructor for help.

5. Once you have the right path going along the mountain range, select the **Type on a Path** ( ) tool. Click and hold on the **Type** ( T ) tool to choose this tool.

6. Click once on the path you just drew and type in the following text: **Introducing**

7. Make that word **38 pt Brush Script Std** and set its color to **Pantone 200**

8. Choose the **Selection** ( ) tool.

**9.** The stroke (and fill if there is one) must be removed.

At the top of the **Swatches** panel:

• Make sure the **Formatting affects container** ( ▣ ) button is selected.

• Make the stroke (or fill) active.

• Click the [None] swatch to remove it.

**10.** Now that you see the type by itself, you may find you want to adjust the path. Go ahead and do it using the **Direct Selection** ( ▸ ) tool.

**11.** When happy with everything, you are ready to print (if you want). Since this document is 10 in by 12 in, you need to print on 11x17 size paper or reduce it to fit on Letter (8.5x11) paper. The following instructions describe how to print.

**12.** If you want, go into **File > Print** and set the following options:

Under **Printer,** choose **[the name of your printer].**

On the left, click on the **Marks and Bleeds** section.
• Check **Crop Marks.**
• Under Bleed and Slug check **Use Document Bleed Settings.**

On the left, click on the **Advanced** section.
• Under **Transparency Flattener** choose **[High Resolution].**

| TO PRINT ON LETTER (8.5X11) PAPER: | TO PRINT ON TABLOID (11X17) PAPER: |
|---|---|
| On the left, click on the **Setup** section. | On the left, click on the **Setup** section. |
| • Under **Paper Size** choose **US Letter.** | • Under **Paper Size** choose **11x17.** |
| • Under **Scale** check **Scale to Fit.** | • Under **Scale** leave Width & Height: **100%.** (Don't check Scale to Fit) |

Look at the Preview on the left to make sure things look OK.
Click **Print.**

**EXERCISE PREVIEW**

**EXERCISE OVERVIEW**

Paragraph and character styles are one of the most important tools you have in InDesign. We show you the basics here, as well as the more advanced and powerful nested styles.

**PREPARING THE FILE**

1.  Open the file **Popcorn.indd.**

    (If you get a message about modified links, click **Update Links.** The exercise file was created on a different computer, but InDesign will automatically find the files for you in their expected folder.)

2.  Do a **File > Save As** and save it as **yourname-popcorn.indd.**

3.  In the **InDesign** menu (MAC) or **Edit** menu (WINDOWS), go to **Preferences > Type.**

4.  Check on **Apply Leading to Entire Paragraphs** and click **OK.**

**IMPORTING THE TEXT**

1.  Choose the **Selection** ( ![cursor] ) tool and select the 4-column text box you see.

2. Do a **File > Place,** and choose **pop.txt.** If you get a missing font alert, do the following instructions, otherwise continue to the next step:

   • Click the **Find Font** button (or if you missed clicking it, go into **Type > Find Font**).

   • At the top, select the missing font (which is probably Times in this case).

   • At the bottom of the window under **Replace With; Font Family** choose **Times** (or any font you have, it really doesn't matter in this case).

   • Click **Change All.**

   • Click **Done.**

### STYLING THE BAND NAME

Typically when starting a design you don't know how you want the text to look, so the first thing you do is style it. Then once you like it, you save that appearance as a style so you can apply it elsewhere. We'll start by styling some of the text.

1. Go into **Type > Show Hidden Characters** so you can see things like Paragraph markers.

2. Select the first word: **Stereolab** (this is a one word paragraph).

3. Make it **14/12.5 Myriad Pro Bold.**

4. We haven't yet defined the color we want. But before we create it, keep the text selected and open the **Swatches** panel **(Window > Color > Swatches).**

5. At the top left of the **Swatches** panel make sure the type's **fill** swatch is in front (active). If it's not, click it to make it active.

6. Go into the **Swatches panel menu** ( 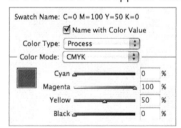 ) and choose **New Color Swatch.**

7. In the window that appears enter the following settings:

| Swatch Name: | C=0 M=100 Y=50 K=0 | |
|---|---|---|
| | ☑ Name with Color Value | |
| Color Type: | Process | |
| Color Mode: | CMYK | |
| Cyan | | 0 % |
| Magenta | | 100 % |
| Yellow | | 50 % |
| Black | | 0 % |

When done with the color click **OK.**

8. The "pink" color swatch (named **C=0 M=100 Y=50 K=0**) you just created is added to the bottom of the panel and has been applied for you.

( **STYLING THE REGULAR TEXT** )

**1.** Select the next **two** paragraphs... from **Dots and Loops** through **Lorraine Ali.**

**2.** Give it the following text attributes:

Font: **Myriad Pro Regular**
Size: **9 pt**
Leading: **12.5 pt**
Alignment: **Justify with last line aligned left** ( ▤ )

**3.** Go into the **Control panel menu** ( ▾☰ ) and choose **Hyphenation.**

**4.** Enter the following settings:

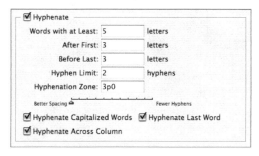

When done click **OK.**

**5.** Go back into the **Control panel menu** ( ▾☰ ) and choose **Justification.**

**6.** Enter the following settings:

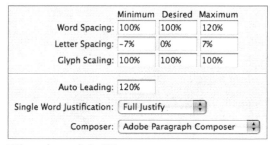

When done click **OK.**

**7.** Select all **three** of the paragraphs you just styled: **Stereolab** through **Lorraine Ali.**

**8.** In the **Control** panel's **Paragraph** ( ¶ ) options click the **Align to Baseline Grid** ( ▤ ) button.

**9.** Select the second line, **Dots and Loops (Elektra).**

**10.** Give it the following attributes:

Font: **Myriad Pro Italic**
Alignment: **Left** ( ▤ )

## CREATING PARAGRAPH STYLES

We're ready to create the styles. Let's start with the band name.

1. Click anywhere in the first paragraph, **Stereolab** (it's only a one word paragraph).

2. Open the **Paragraph Styles** panel **(Type > Paragraph Styles)**.

3. Go into the **Paragraph Styles panel menu** ( ▾☰ ) and choose **New Paragraph Style.**

4. Name this one **Band Name** and click **OK.**

   NOTE: You didn't have to set anything in the style sheet since InDesign copied all of the settings from the paragraph the cursor was in!

5. Let's create another style for the album info. Click anywhere in the second line. This is a one line paragraph that reads: **Dots and Loops (Elektra).**

6. In the **Paragraph Styles panel menu** ( ▾☰ ) choose **New Paragraph Style.**

7. Name this one **Album Info** and click **OK.**

8. One more style for the regular text—click anywhere in the large paragraph below that. It begins "Stereolab take their..."

9. In the **Paragraph Styles panel menu** ( ▾☰ ) choose **New Paragraph Style.**

   TIP: A faster way to create a style is to hold **Option** ⓂⒶⒸ or **Alt** ⓌⒾⓃⒹⓄⓌⓈ and click the **New Style** ( ▯ ) button at the bottom of the panel. (If you don't hold **Alt/Option** while clicking the button InDesign will give the style a generic name.)

10. Name this one **Body** and click **OK.**

## APPLYING THE STYLES

While we have created our styles, none of the text is using them yet. Let's start by applying the **Body** style to all the text.

1. Make sure the cursor is sitting somewhere in the text frame.

2. Go to **Edit > Select All.**

3. In the **Paragraph Styles** panel click on the **Body** style to apply it.

4. Click anywhere in the first paragraph **(Stereolab).**

5. Click on the **Band Name** style to apply it.

   NOTE: You technically do not have to select the whole paragraph when applying a paragraph style. Paragraph styles must apply to the entire paragraph.

6. Find the next band name **(Photek)** and click anywhere in it.

7. Click on the **Band Name** style to apply it.

**8.** Continue styling the rest of the **Band Names.**
Here are the remaining names in case you can't spot 'em.

| | | |
|---|---|---|
| **Tanya Donelly** | **Helium** | **Steve Earle** |
| **Boyz II Men** | **The Sundays** | **Matraca Berg** |

**9.** Under each of the band names is the short (often one line) paragraph for the **Album Info.** Apply the **Album Info** to each of those paragraphs.

## CHANGING STYLES ONCE THEY'VE BEEN CREATED

It would look better if there were more space between the bands. Let's add some space above the band name. Since we have a style sheet for the band names we'll just change it and all the band names will be updated.

**1.** Make sure nothing is selected **(Edit > Deselect All).**

**2.** In the **Paragraph Styles** panel double-click **Band Name.**

**3.** Click on the **Indents and Spacing** section on the left.

**4.** Set **Space Before** to **1p** and click **OK.**

**5.** All the band names should now have more space before them.

## OPTICAL MARGIN ALIGNMENT

**1.** Before we continue working with our styles, let's improve the alignment of the left/right edges of the columns. With the text cursor still in the text box (or as long as the box is still selected) go into **Type > Story.**

**2.** In the **Story** panel that opens set the following:
• check **Optical Margin Alignment**
• set it to **12 pt** (this setting is typically the same as your type size, or close to it)

This hangs roman punctuation like quotes, periods, etc. a bit outside the column so the column "visually" looks better justified.

## CREATING & APPLYING A CHARACTER STYLE

**1.** At the end of each review is the name of the reviewer.
Select the first reviewer, **Lorraine Ali.**

**2.** In the **Control** panel make it **8 pt** and **All Caps** TT

**3.** Since this text isn't the whole paragraph it can't be a **paragraph** style, it must be a **character** style. With the text still selected go to the **Character Styles** panel **(Type > Character Styles).**

**4.** From the **Character Styles panel menu** ( ▾≡ ) choose **New Character Style.**

**5.** Don't click OK till we say so! Name this one **Reviewer.**

**6.** Click in the **Shortcut** field.

**7.** Hold **Shift** and on your keyboard's number pad (the numbers on the right of the keyboard, NOT at the top) hit number **1**. Don't have a number pad? Read the note to the right.

In the field you'll see **Shift+Num 1** appear. That means you can use that key combination to quickly apply this style sheet.

**8.** Click **OK** to close the Style Options window.

NOTE: Just like it did before, InDesign looked at the selected text and copied the formatting into the style.

**9.** With the **Lorraine Ali** text still selected, in the **Character Styles** panel click on **Reviewer** to apply the style.

NOTE: The text won't look different but it will be linked to the style now.

**10.** Go through the text and apply the **Reviewer** style to each reviewer. If you want to do this fast, just select the name, hold **Shift** and hit the number **1** on the number keypad. This will apply the style instantly. (If your keyboard does not have a number pad will need to click on the **Reviewer** style in the **Character Styles** panel instead.)

NOTE: If you can't see the last article's reviewer you can come back to that in a little while once we've fit the text.

### CREATING A NESTED CHARACTER STYLE

**1.** Look at the second line of text: **Dots and Loops (Elektra).**

**2.** The text before the parentheses is the title of the CD. Select just the text **Dots and Loops.**

**3.** Make it **Myriad Pro Semibold.**

**4.** Let's turn this into a style sheet so we can apply it to the other CD titles. Since this text isn't the whole paragraph it can't be a paragraph style, it must be a character style. Make sure the **Dots and Loops** text is still selected.

**5.** Open the **Character Styles** panel **(Type > Character Styles).**

**6.** From the **Character Styles panel menu** ( ▾≡ ) choose **New Character Style.**

**7.** Name this one **CD Title** and click **OK.**

---

**NO NUMBER PAD?**

Some keyboards that do not have a separate number pad have a one overlaid on the **J, K, L,** etc. keys. The **Fn** key gives you access to it. Sadly not all do (newer Mac laptops removed the overlaid number pad) so you can't use keystrokes to apply styles without connecting a full keyboard. If you have an overlaid number pad, the keystroke would be **Shift–Fn–J** (which should have a **1** next to it.) You must press the keys in that order! **Shift,** then **Fn,** then **J!**

8. Before applying this style, let's take a closer look. At the start of each **Album Info** line there is always the name of the CD (they appear before the labels in parentheses). While we could select each one and manually apply the **CD Title** style ourselves, there is an easier way. Since the text always follows a pattern of: **CD Title (label)** ...we can have InDesign style the text up to the first parenthesis for us! To do this we will "nest" the **CD Title** character style into the **Album Info** style that has already been applied to that text. Let's do that now.

9. Deselect everything by choosing **Edit > Deselect All.**

10. In the **Paragraph Styles** panel double-click the **Album Info** style.

11. On the left, click on the **Drop Caps and Nested Styles** section.

12. Click the **New Nested Style** button and set the following options:

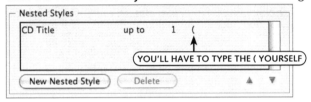

13. Click **OK** and check it out. All the CD Titles are now styled for you!

**( SPACE BEFORE REVIEWERS )**

1. Notice that all the reviewer names have tabs before them. The reviewer names should align right, so we are going to change these tabs. Here's a nifty way to do it:

   **If the name is on the same line as other text:**
   • Select the actual tab character (we don't want it anymore so we'll replace it).
   • Then type in a **Shift–Tab** (this is a right aligned tab).

   **If the name is on a line by itself:**
   • Click to the left of the name and type a **Shift–Tab** (this is a right aligned tab).

2. Repeat the above step until you've put a **Shift–Tab** before every author.

3. We can't style the last reviewer because the text is not all fitting. Let's fix that.

**( FITTING THE TEXT )**

1. Now that we have styled everything we need to get all the text to fit and then break nicely. We'll be using tracking, and its default keystroke amount is too large. To fix it, go into the **InDesign** menu (**MAC**) or **Edit** menu (**WINDOWS**), and choose **Preferences > Units & Increments.**

2. Change **Kerning/Tracking** to **5** and click **OK.**

3. Look at the end of each review. If the reviewer is on its own line it probably looks fine, such as with the first three reviews.

   Other reviews such as for the band **Helium,** have awkward breaks. The reviewer **Matt Diehl** has just his last name hanging in the top of the fourth column. To fix this we'll "cheat" by tracking the text:

   • Select the entire paragraph of the review.
   • Try tracking it in using **Option–left arrow** (MAC) or **Alt–left arrow** (WINDOWS).
     (Do not do this more than three times for a total tracking of -15 as more than that will be too noticeable.) That should bring the reviewer's name all on to one line.
   • Try tracking text in or out on other paragraphs as needed to fill the spaces until the bottom of each review looks nicely filled out. If you find a paragraph where too much text spills onto the last line, try tracking only part of the paragraph instead of all of it.

4. That last reviewer, **Henry Cabot Beck,** should now fit at the end of the text frame.

   • Select it.
   • Apply the **Reviewer** character style.
   • Put a **Shift–Tab** in front of it.
   • Apply any tracking you think it needs to look good.

5. That's it, you're done! Now these styles can be used for all future issues that use this format for CD reviews.

### GETTING STARTED

*Zooming*

*Scrolling*

*Getting Around*

*Tools*

*Copy & Paste*

### PHOTO RETOUCHING

*Selections*

*Healing Brush*

*Clone Stamp*

*Red-Eye tool*

### REPLACING BACKGROUNDS

*Magic Wand*

*Image Compositing*

### ANNUAL REPORT COVER

*Selecting*

*Feathering*

*Layers*

*Using Type*

### SELECTING WITH QUICK MASKS

*Quick Masks*

*Magic Wand*

### CROPPING, RESIZING, AND BLENDING

*Patterns*

*Selections*

*Gradient Tool*

*Continued…*

### PREPARING DIGITAL PHOTOS FOR PRINT

*Image Size*

*Resampling*

*Saving as PSD*

*Saving as TIFF*

*Document Size*

*Preparing for Print*

### SAVING PHOTOS FOR THE WEB AS JPEG

*Saving for the Web*

*Save as JPEG*

*Image Size*

*Resampling*

### SAVING WEB GRAPHICS AS GIF/PNG

*Comparing GIF and PNG*

*Web Transparency*

### ADJUSTMENT LAYERS AND MASKS

*Color Correction with Adjustment Layers*

*Layer Masks*

*Curves*

*Hue/Saturation*

### USING LAYER MASKS FOR SILHOUETTES

*Layer Masks*

*Selection Techniques*

*Magnetic Lasso*

*Refine Edge*

*Color Fill*

### EXERCISE OVERVIEW

In this exercise, you'll start learning the basics of viewing/navigating around images and some basic Photoshop tools.

### ( GETTING STARTED )

1. Launch **Photoshop.**

2. Go to **File > Open** and:
   – Navigate to the **Desktop**.
   – Go into the **Class Files** folder.
   – Then go into the **Photoshop Class** folder.
   – Open the file **Guy.psd.**

### ( RESTORING PHOTOSHOP'S DEFAULT SETTINGS )

Since you (or other people on your computer) may have already experimented with Photoshop we want to make sure it's reset to the default settings.

1. Go to **Window > Workspace > Photography.**

2. **Mac** users only, go into the **Window** menu. If **Application Frame** is not checked, choose it to turn on the application frame**.**

3. As shown below, in the **Options** bar at the top of the screen, on the far left you will see a button that shows the currently selected tool.

4. **Ctrl–click** (MAC) or **Right-click** (WINDOWS) on that button.

5. From the menu that appears, choose **Reset All Tools** and click **OK.**

### ( NAVIGATING AN IMAGE—ZOOMING AND SCROLLING )

1. In the Toolbox click on the **Zoom** ( 🔍 ) tool.

2. In the image, position the cursor over the guy's head and click once to zoom in.

3. To zoom out again, hold **Option** (MAC) or **Alt** (WINDOWS) and click once to zoom out.

4.  To zoom in more quickly, in the **Options** bar, **UN**check Scrubby Zoom if it's not already grayed out.

5.  Drag a box over the area you want to see and then release the mouse.

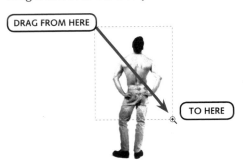

DRAG FROM HERE

TO HERE

6.  To see the whole image again, choose **View > Fit on Screen.**

7.  Instead of using the **Zoom** ( 🔍 ) tool we can also use keystrokes:
    *   To zoom **in** press **Cmd–plus(+)** ⒨ or **Ctrl–plus(+)** ⓦⒾⓃⒹⓄⓌⓈ.
    *   To zoom **out** press **Cmd–minus(-)** ⒨ or **Ctrl–minus(-)** ⓦⒾⓃⒹⓄⓌⓈ.

8.  Zoom in a few times so you only see a portion of the image.

9.  To scroll around the image, hold the **Spacebar** and drag anywhere on the image. When done, let go of the mouse and the Spacebar.

10. To see the whole image again, choose **View > Fit on Screen.**

> ## SCRUBTASTIC ZOOMING
>
> **Scrubby Zoom** was one of the new features introduced in Photoshop CS5. To use it, check **Scrubby Zoom** on in the **Options** bar. Click and hold over the area you would like to zoom into and, in a scrubbing motion, drag the mouse to the right to zoom in. To zoom out, scrub to the left. Let go of the mouse when you have zoomed to the desired level. That's all there is to it. Scrub on!
>
> NOTE: Not all computers can support this feature. If it is grayed out in the options bar, then your computer cannot use Scrubby Zoom.

## USING A PAINT BRUSH

1.  In the Toolbox, choose the **Brush** ( ✏ ) tool.

2.  As shown below, at the bottom of the Toolbox click on the **Foreground** color swatch.

CLICK THE COLOR SWATCH —

3.  In the window that opens, choose a color as shown below.

#1: DRAG UP/DOWN TO CHANGE COLORS

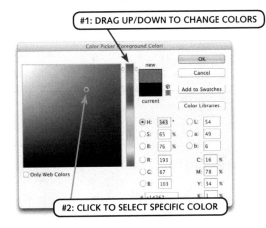

#2: CLICK TO SELECT SPECIFIC COLOR

4. Click **OK.**

5. Drag anywhere on the image to paint with the brush.

6. Let's change the brush color. Towards the bottom of the Toolbox click the **Default Colors** (  ) icon to set the Foreground color to black and the Background color to white.

CLICK TO SET DEFAULT COLORS ——

7. Let's change the brush as well. As shown below, in the **Options** bar at the top of screen, click on the **Brush Preset picker.**

8. Use the sliders to change the **Size** and **Hardness.**

9. Drag anywhere on the image to paint with the new brush.

10. While **Edit > Undo** can undo the very last step, to undo more steps we need to use the **History** panel. Open the **History** panel by going to **Window > History.**

11. Click on the step **before** the **Brush Tool.** This undoes all the brushing.

CLICK ON THE STEP BEFORE THE BRUSH TOOL TO UNDO THE BRUSHING

## BASIC SELECTIONS & COPY/PASTE

1. In the Toolbox on the left, choose the **Rectangular Marquee** ( ▣ ) tool.

2. In the image, drag a selection box that encompasses the entire guy.

3. Choose the **Move** ( ▸⊕ ) tool.

4. Drag anywhere inside the selection and move the guy more to the left.

5. Since the guy is already selected, we'd like to make a copy of him. But before we do, on the right of the screen, look in the **Layers** panel to see there's only a **Background** layer.

6. Do an **Edit > Copy.**

7. Do an **Edit > Paste.**

8. You won't see major changes in the image, but look in the **Layers** panel on the right to see a new layer named **Layer 1.**

9. Drag the guy to move him. Now you'll be able to see you are moving the copy!

10. We don't need this copy, so let's delete it. As shown on the right, in the **Layers** panel, drag **Layer 1** to the **Trash** ( 🗑 ) button at the bottom right of the panel.

### USING THE CLONE STAMP TOOL

Using the Clone Stamp is like copying and pasting, but on the same layer. In later exercises you'll come to see it's a powerful retouching tool. Let's see how it works.

1. In the Toolbox, choose the **Clone Stamp** ( 🔲 ) tool.

2. Position the cursor over the thing you want to copy. In this case, the guy's head.

3. **Option–Click** (MAC) or **Alt–Click** (WINDOWS) to target it as the source area to be copied.

4. If you're still holding Alt/Option, let go of it now.

5. Move the cursor to the white area to the guy's right, where we want to paste. Notice the cool preview. It's awesome.

6. **Click and drag** with the mouse to paint. The head you targeted in the last step will be pasted here.
NOTE: If you continue to drag down, you'll see the guy's neck and shoulder also appear. Keep that in mind

7. That's it for our Photoshop warm up. You can close the image without saving the changes.

**EXERCISE PREVIEW**

BEFORE

AFTER

**EXERCISE OVERVIEW**

In this exercise, you'll perform common retouching tasks: eliminating red eye, erasing facial blemishes, and removing an undesired background element.

1. Go to **File > Open.**

2. Navigate to the **Desktop,** go into the **Class Files** folder, then the **Photoshop Class** folder, and open the file **WaynesWorld.tif.**

## FIXING BLEMISHES

1. We're going to touch up the blemishes in their faces, so zoom in to get a better look. You can do this by choosing the **Zoom** ( 🔍 ) tool and clicking on the image, or by pressing **Cmd–plus(+)** (MAC) or **Ctrl–plus(+)** (WINDOWS) .

2. Choose the **Healing Brush** ( 🖊 ) tool. (You may have to click and hold the **Spot Healing Brush** ( 🖊 ) tool to see it.)

3. We need a small, soft brush, so go to the **Options** bar at the top of the screen and click on the **Brush Preset picker.**

4. In the pop-up panel, set Size to **6 px** and Hardness to **60%.**
Close the panel when done.

5. The **Healing Brush** ( 🖊 ) requires two steps:
   – **Option–Click** (MAC) or **Alt–Click** (WINDOWS) on a good area of the face to set where you are sampling from.
   – Move the cursor over a blemish, and click to fix it.

   HINT: Because you are working with skin textures/tones that change over the face, it's a good idea to **Option–Click** (MAC) or **Alt–Click** (WINDOWS) fairly close to the blemish so that you get the same general texture/tone.

6. Find another blemish on the faces and repeat the process:
   – **Option–Click** (MAC) or **Alt–Click** (WINDOWS) on a good area with no facial blemishes.
   – Then click on the blemish (or click and drag to affect a broader area).

   Once you've eliminated a few imperfections, move on to the next step.

7. Choose **View > Actual Pixels** to see the best representation of the image's quality for print or web.

8. When you are happy with the image, go into **File > Save As.**
   – From the **Format** menu, choose **Photoshop.**
   – If you're not already in the **Photoshop Class** folder, navigate into it.
   – Name the file **yourname-WaynesWorld.psd**
   – Click **Save.**

## REMOVING THE HAND

1. To remove Wayne's hand, we must completely cover it over with sky. The **Clone Stamp** ( ▣ ) tool is best suited for this, so choose it now.

   NOTE: You use the **Healing Brush** ( ▣ ) and **Clone Stamp** ( ▣ ) exactly the same way, but the Clone Stamp "clones" an area exactly (almost like copying and pasting), whereas the Healing Brush "heals" an area by melding the textures from the source and the tones from the destination (where you paint).

2. In the **Options** bar at the top of the screen, click on the **Brush Preset picker.**

3. Set the Size to **35 px** and Hardness to **0%.** Close the panel when you're done.

4. **Option–Click** (MAC) or **Alt–Click** (WINDOWS) in the clouds/sky to define the source that you'll be copying. Along the right side you'll want to sample blue sky, and along the left you will sample the cloud.

5. Move the cursor over the hand, and click and drag on the hand to clone onto that area. Because the background varies in tone, you'll need to **Option–Click** (MAC) or **Alt–Click** (WINDOWS) in different parts of the clouds/sky to sample different tones to create something that looks natural.

6. As you near the bottom of the hand, you may have to clone over the top edge of Garth's hair to get rid of all of the hand. Don't worry; you will add more hair later.

7. The edge of your cloud may be a bit even and abrupt compared to the original background clouds. To get a varied edge, go to the **Options** bar at the top of the screen and set the Opacity to **20%.**

8. Also in the **Options** bar, click on the **Brush Preset picker** and select a somewhat small, soft-edged brush. (**13 px** with a Hardness of **0%** is good.)

9. **Option–Click** (MAC) or **Alt–Click** (WINDOWS) in the cloud to sample from it.

10. Then click along the edge of the cloud to get a bit more variation.

### FIXING THE HAIR

Now that you've covered the hand with sky, the top of Garth's head probably looks a bit rough. Let's patch up the hair with the **Clone Stamp** ( ) tool.

1. Select the **Clone Stamp** ( ) and in the **Options** bar:
   – Select a small, soft brush. (Around **10 px** should work.)
   – Set the Opacity to **100%.**

2. Look at the top of Garth's head to determine the overall color and direction of the missing hair. **Option–Click** (MAC) or **Alt–Click** (WINDOWS) on a section of the remaining hair that matches these characteristics.

3. Click and drag along the top of Garth's head to clone over the missing hair.

4. If it doesn't look quite right, try sampling a different area instead:
   – **Option–Click** (MAC) or **Alt–Click** (WINDOWS) on the hair you like.
   – Then click and drag on the hair you don't like.
   – You'll probably get the best results by sampling several different areas.

### ELIMINATING RED-EYE

Finally, it's time to get rid of Wayne's irritating red-eye problem. Luckily we have a tool specifically for this.

1. Choose the **Zoom** ( ) tool and zoom in on Wayne's face.

2. Click and hold on the **Healing Brush** ( ) tool and choose the **Red Eye** ( ) tool.

3. Click once in the red part of Wayne's eye. Voila! The red eye is gone.

4. Click again on the other eye to fix it.

5. If you want, you can save the file.

   Congratulations—you've completed your first retouching job!

**EXERCISE PREVIEW**

**EXERCISE OVERVIEW**

In this exercise, you'll combine two separate photos. The first image features a man against a boring background. To make the composition more interesting, you'll cut him out (often called "silhouetting") and place him in front of the second image.

1. Go to **File > Open.**

   From the **Photoshop Class** folder, open the files **baseball.jpg** and **security.tif.**

2. Make sure **security.tif** is the active document.

3. From the Toolbox, choose the **Magic Wand** (  ) tool. If you don't see it, click and hold on the **Quick Selection** ( ) tool and then choose it.

   NOTE: The Magic Wand is a selection tool that recognizes color variations. When you click on an area of the image with the Magic Wand, all adjacent areas of similar color will be selected.

4. In the **Options** bar, set the **Tolerance** to **20.** This makes the magic wand less picky about which colors are similar enough to be part of the selection. Lower numbers means fewer colors, and therefore less of the image will be selected.

5. Click on part of the green background. You'll find that a large part of it becomes selected, but that there are many parts of the background that are not yet selected.

6. Go to the **Options** bar at the top of the screen. Near the left, you'll find a row of four similar icons. Currently, the first icon, **New selection** ( ), is highlighted. Click on the second icon, **Add to selection** ( ).

7. Click on another section of the green background. The original selection remains and a new selection is added to it.

8. Continue clicking on the green background until all of it is selected. Don't forget the areas between the railings!

   NOTE: If part of the man or the railings becomes selected, just use **Cmd–Z** (MAC) or **Ctrl–Z** (WINDOWS) to undo your most recent step. Then try clicking on a different section of the background with the **Magic Wand** ( 🪄 ) tool. You can also change the Tolerance to a lower number to make the Magic Wand pickier.

9. Choose **Select > Inverse.** Instead of having the background selected, you now have everything *except* the background selected.

10. Use **Cmd–C** (MAC) or **Ctrl–C** (WINDOWS) to **copy** the selected area.

11. Go into the **Window** menu and choose **baseball.jpg** to make it the active document.

12. Use **Cmd–V** (MAC) or **Ctrl–V** (WINDOWS) to **paste** the **copied** image onto this image.

13. Go to your **Layers** panel. If it's not already open, use the **Window** menu to open it.

   Notice that the content that you've pasted has been automatically placed onto a new layer named **Layer 1.**

14. **Double-click** directly on the name **Layer 1** and rename it **security.** Hit **Return** (MAC) or **Enter** (WINDOWS) to apply.

15. From the Toolbox, choose the **Move** ( ⊹ ) tool.

16. Drag the security guard down or up to line up his bottom edge with the bottom of the document.

### ( CLEANING UP )

1. You may find that tiny bits of the green background show up at some of the guard's edges.

2. From the Toolbox, choose the **Eraser** ( 🧽 ) tool.

3. In the **Options** bar, choose a fairly small, hard-edged brush. (Try **8 px.**)

4. Use the **Eraser** to carefully brush over the green bits on the edges of the guard's sleeves. (It will help to zoom in for this part.)

   Note that the areas of the security layer that you've erased become transparent.

5. When you're satisfied with the results, do a **File > Save As.**
   – Set **Format** to **Photoshop.**
   – Name it **yourname-baseball.psd**
   – If it asks you if you want to **Maximize Compatibility,** just leave it checked and click **OK.**

NOTE: Most of the Photoshop class files have been saved as JPEG documents to conserve file size, but you'll always want to save the master copy of your image as a Photoshop Document (.psd). This ensures that the image retains the maximum amount of editability, such as multiple layers. It also maintains the image's quality. JPEG compression reduces the image quality in order to make the file smaller.

---

### TO MAXIMIZE OR NOT TO MAXIMIZE?

By default, Photoshop is set to ask whether you want to **Maximize Compatibility** of Photoshop documents. If you choose to **Maximize Compatibility:**
• The document will be more compatible with older versions of Photoshop.
• The file size may be larger.
• You should maximize compatibility if working with Adobe InDesign.

If you choose NOT to **Maximize Compatibility:**
• The document will not be as compatible with older versions of Photoshop.
• The file size may be smaller.

To turn off that annoying reminder once and for all, go to **Photoshop > Preferences > File Handling** (MAC) or **Edit > Preferences > File Handling** (WINDOWS) and under **Maximize PSD and PSB File Compatibility** choose either **Never** or **Always** and click **OK.**

**EXERCISE PREVIEW**

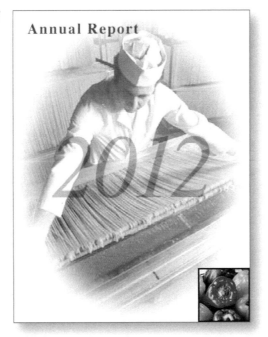

**EXERCISE OVERVIEW**

This exercise will give you practice making selections, feathering selections, copying from file to file, adding type, and using layer opacity.

### DESATURATING THE BACKGROUND TO MAKE THE PASTA "POP"

1. In the **Photoshop Class** folder, open the file **Report Cover.jpg**.

2. To enlarge the image on screen, go to **View > Fit on Screen**.
   This will make it easy to do the fine selection work we're about to do.

3. As shown below, in the **Layers** panel, click and drag the **Background** layer down to the **New Layer** ( ) icon at the bottom right. This creates a duplicate layer that we can edit without changing the original image.

4. Click on the **Polygonal Lasso** ( ) tool. If you don't see it, click and hold on the **Lasso** ( ) tool and then choose it.

5. Click on a corner of the tray of spaghetti between the man's arms, then move to another corner and click again. Continue clicking on corners until you've returned to your first corner. Click on that corner or hit **Enter** (or **Return**) to complete the pasta selection.

6. Once you have the whole tray selected, go into **Select > Modify > Feather.**

7. Set the **Feather Radius** to **2** pixels and click **OK.** This softens the edge of the selection slightly so our adjustment will blend at the edge.

8. Go to the **Select** menu and choose **Inverse.**

9. Go into **Image > Adjustments > Hue/Saturation.**
   – Change the **Saturation** by typing **–75** in its field (that's negative 75!).
   – Change the **Lightness** by typing **25** in its field.

   Click **OK.**

10. Deselect the selection using **Cmd–D** (MAC) or **Ctrl–D** (WINDOWS).

## ( ADDING A SOFT OVAL FRAME )

1. If the rulers are not already showing, go into the **View** menu and select **Rulers.**

2. If the rulers aren't in inches, **Ctrl–click** (MAC) or **Right-click** (WINDOWS) in the ruler and choose **Inches** from the menu.

3. Go to **View > Actual Pixels.** The rulers should now have a tick mark every 0.125″.

4. Go to the **View** menu, and make sure that **Snap** is checked.

5. Select the **Move** ( ) tool.

   NOTE: To move a guide after it's set into place, you must use the **Move** ( ) tool.

6. Position the mouse over the left ruler. You are going to pull a guide out by clicking and dragging from the ruler. Hold **Shift** (to make the guides snap into place at the tick), then click and drag the mouse so that a guide is positioned **0.375″** inside the left edge. (That's 3 ruler tick marks from the edge.)

7. Pull another guide down from the top ruler and position it **0.375″** inside the top edge.

8. Pull out two more guides so that they are **0.375″** in from the right and bottom edges.

9. Choose the **Elliptical Marquee** ( ) tool. (If you don't see it, click and hold on the **Rectangular Marquee** ( ), then choose it.)

10. Position the mouse at the intersection of the top and left guides.

11. Click and drag to draw an oval selection to the intersection of the guides at the bottom right of the image.

12. In the **Options** bar at the top of the screen, click the **Refine Edge** button and:
    – Hold **Option** (MAC) or **Alt** (WINDOWS) to have the Cancel button switch to the Reset button, and click the **Reset** button.
    – In the **Adjust Edge** section, change **Feather** to **15 px**.
    – Behind the Refine Edge dialog you should see a preview of this feathered edge on a white background.
    – Click **OK**.

13. The selection will now appear as a line of "marching ants," as they are often referred to. Even though it may not look like it, don't worry; the selection is still feathered.

14. From the **Select** menu, choose **Inverse**.

15. If it isn't already showing, open the **Layers** panel **(Window > Layers)**.

16. To fill the oval frame we'll use a fill layer since its color can later be easily changed. As shown to the right, at the bottom of the **Layers** panel, click the **Create new fill or adjustment layer** (  ) button, and from the menu, choose **Solid Color**.

17. In the Color Picker that appears, choose **White** and click **OK**.

18. **Double-click** directly on the layer's name and rename it **Oval Frame**. Hit **Return** (MAC) or **Enter** (WINDOWS) to apply.

19. Hide the guides from view by choosing **View > Show > Guides**.

## ADDING THE PEPPER PICTURE

1. From the **Photoshop Class** folder, open the **Red Pepper.psd** file.

2. Make sure **Red Pepper.psd** and **Report Cover.jpg** are the only two documents you have open. If you have any others open, close them now.

3. Go to **Window > Arrange > 2-Up Vertical** so you can see both pictures next to each other.

4. Choose the **Move** ( ) tool.

5. Drag the **red pepper** image into the **Report Cover** window and let go of the mouse.

6. Close **Red Pepper.psd**.

7. You should now be back in the **Report Cover** file. Look in the **Layers** panel and notice a new **Layer 1** has been created.

8. In the **Layers** panel, **double-click** directly on the name **Layer 1**. Rename it **Pepper** and hit **Return** (MAC) or **Enter** (WINDOWS).

9. Use the **Move** ( ) tool and bring the image to the lower right corner. It should snap into place when you get close. Otherwise, you can use the arrow keys to fine tune the placement.

**10.** The pepper image would stand out better if it had a thin black line around it. At the bottom of the **Layers** panel, click the **Add a layer style** ( *fx.* ) button and from the menu, choose **Stroke.**

**11.** Set the following options:

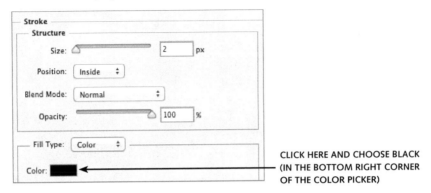

CLICK HERE AND CHOOSE BLACK
(IN THE BOTTOM RIGHT CORNER
OF THE COLOR PICKER)

When done, click **OK.**

### ADDING THE TYPE

**1.** Choose the **Type** ( T ) tool.

**2.** In the **Options** bar at the top of the screen, click the **Color** swatch.

CLICK HERE

**3.** Move the dialog that appears so you can see the red pepper. Mouse over the pepper and notice that the cursor turns into the **Eyedropper** ( ) tool. Click with the **Eyedropper** ( ) to sample the red from the pepper.

Click **OK.**

**4.** You will be back in the **Type** ( T ) tool. Position the cursor somewhere near the top lefthand corner, then click.

**5.** Type in the words **Annual Report.**

**6.** Highlight the text and in the **Options** bar at the top of the screen set the following:
– **Times Bold** (Choose **Times** from the 1st menu, and **Bold** from the 2nd menu.)
– Font Size ( ): **20** pts (You'll need to type this number in the font size field.)
– Anti-Aliasing ( ): **Crisp**

**7.** In order to track out the letters, you must open the **Character** panel. You can choose **Window > Character** or click the **Panels** ( ) button on the right of the **Options** bar.

Set the **Tracking** ( ) to **140.**

8.  When done with the type, click the **checkbox** ( ✓ ) toward the right side of the **Options** bar. (If it's not there, don't worry—Photoshop already automatically applied the changes for you.)

9.  In the **Layers** panel, you should now see a layer named **Annual Report.** This layer has a "T" thumbnail image ( T ) to indicate that it is a type layer.

10. Select the **Move** ( ) tool and move the type so it starts about ¼" from the top and about ⅛" from the left.

11. Choose the **Type** ( T ) tool again.

12. Click in the center of the image and type **2012**

13. Highlight the text and make it:
    – Times Italic
    – Font Size ( ) : **120** pts

14. In the **Character** panel **(Window > Character)**:
    – Click the swatch next to **Color** and in the window that appears, choose **black.** Click **OK.**
    – Set the **Tracking** ( ) to **0.**

15. Using the **Move** ( ) tool, position the type so it's nicely centered on the image.

16. You'll notice that in the **Layers** panel, a new type layer named **2012** is highlighted. Above the layer name, near the top of the panel, is the **Opacity** of that layer. Change it to **40%.**

17. Do a **File > Save As.**

18. Set **Format** to **Photoshop**.
    Name the file **yourname-Report Cover.psd** and click **Save.**
    NOTE: Saving as a Photoshop document (.psd) file will save all layers and editable items like type.

**EXERCISE PREVIEW**

**EXERCISE OVERVIEW**

Often, selecting part of an image proves too intricate for conventional selection tools. Quick Mask Mode allows you to use painting tools to create or refine selections, allowing for greater precision.

## STARTING THE SELECTION USING TRADITIONAL SELECTION TOOLS

1. From the **Photoshop Class** folder, open the file **watchingSailboat.tif.**

2. Choose the **Magic Wand** ( ![icon] ) tool.

3. In the **Options** bar:
   – Set the **Tolerance** to **32.** (This is the Magic Wand's default setting.)
   – Click **Add to selection** ( ![icon] ).

4. Click on part of the water and trees around the man and girl.

5. Continue clicking on the area around the man and girl until most of it is selected.
   – Focus on getting the best selection you can around the man and girl.
     But don't worry if it's not perfect—we'll be finishing it in the following steps.
   – It's OK if you miss a few spots in the background. That's easy to fix later.

6. Go to **Select > Inverse.** (Now the people are selected, rather than the area around them.)

### REFINING THE SELECTION IN QUICK MASK MODE

**1.** As shown below, in the Toolbox there's an **Edit in Quick Mask Mode** ( 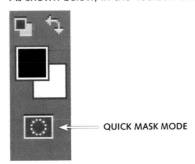 ) button.

QUICK MASK MODE

**2.** Double-click the **Quick Mask Mode** ( ) button to set its display options.

**3.** In the dialog that opens, choose Color Indicates: **Selected Areas** and click **OK**.

NOTE: You're now in Quick Mask Mode, where your selection is indicated by colored shading instead of the marching ants dotted outline. In this mode, we can change the selection by painting with **black** to **select** and painting with **white** to **deselect.** You won't see black and white as you paint, though. Painting with **black** should appear as **red** unless the color was changed in the Quick Mask Options dialog you were just in. Painting with **white** would remove the color, indicating the area will be **deselected.**

**4.** We want to **add** to our selection so we need to be painting with **black.** As shown to the right, in the Toolbox, click the **Default Colors** ( ) icon to make sure the **Foreground** color is pure **black.**

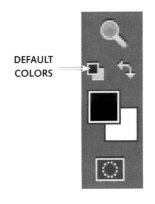

DEFAULT
COLORS

**5.** Choose the **Brush** ( ) tool and in the **Options** bar:
  – Pick a **large, hard-edged brush.**
  – Set the Opacity and Flow to **100%.**

**6.** Most of the man and girl are shaded already, but you may have missed some pieces:
  – Completely shade in the large solid areas of the man and girl. We'll get to the edge details in a few steps.
  – Don't worry about the background for now.

NOTE: You're painting with **black,** which adds shading, therefore **selecting** them.

**7.** Press the **X** key on your keyboard to swap the **Foreground** and **Background** colors.

**8.** You're now painting with **white,** which removes shading, therefore **deselecting.** Paint over any areas of the background to remove the colored shading.

**9.** Check the other edges of the man and the girl. Where necessary:
  – Paint with **white** to **deselect** (remove the shading).
  – Paint with **black** to **select** (add shading).
  – Soft brushes may work better for hair edges, but you'll probably want hard brushes for everything else.
  – To create a feathered look for the wispy hair, you may want to reduce the opacity of your brush in the **Options** bar.

10. You should now be finished painting the selection. In the Toolbox, click the **Edit in Standard Mode** ( ) button shown to the right.

    The shading has become a selection!

11. Double-check the selection for little spots you may have missed (the "marching ants" at selection edges should make it obvious). If you've missed an area, go back into **Quick Mask Mode** to correct it, then return to **Standard Mode**.

    NOTE: Quick Mask Mode is *only* for making selections, and will not allow you to edit the image at all. Always return to **Standard Mode** when you've finished making a selection in **Quick Mask Mode**.

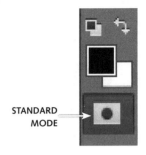

STANDARD
MODE

### ( PUTTING THE PEOPLE ONTO A NEW BACKGROUND )

1. Go to **Select > Modify > Contract.**

2. Enter a value of **1** and click **OK.**

3. Use **Cmd–C** (MAC) or **Ctrl–C** (WINDOWS) to **copy** the selected area.

4. Go to **File > Open,** and from the **Photoshop Class** folder, open the file **shore.tif.**

5. Use **Cmd–V** (MAC) or **Ctrl–V** (WINDOWS) to **paste** the **copied** image onto this image.

6. Use the **Move** ( ) tool to position them in the new picture.

    This looks a little awkward since the light on the people is from the left, but the light on the landscape is from the right.

7. Go to **Edit > Transform > Flip Horizontal.**

8. Reposition them on the left of the image as needed.

    Much better! Now the light sources match fairly well.
    And the people have a crisp, precise silhouette, thanks to Quick Mask Mode!

9. If you like, save the file as **yourname-watching the shore.psd.**

**EXERCISE PREVIEW**

**EXERCISE OVERVIEW**

This exercise shows you the gradient tool and how to apply fills with special blending options such as "multiply." It also reviews selections and patterns.

**CLEANING UP THE BACKGROUND**

1. From the **Photoshop Class** folder, open **Riddick Bowe.tif**.

2. Select the **Crop** ( 🔲 ) tool.

3. Notice how the whole image is selected, with handles in all four corners and on all four sides. Simply click on the handle at the right, and crop out the "BUDW" sign. You can also click and drag in the middle to move the whole cropping area.

4. Once the crop is placed correctly, do any **one** of the following:
   – Click the **checkbox** ( ✅ ) at the right in the **Options** bar.
   – Hit **Return** (MAC) or **Enter** (WINDOWS).
   – **Double-click** inside the cropped area.

5. We want all of the black background around Riddick to be of the same tone. It currently varies slightly, and it's not a truly solid black. We'll fill it with a solid color, but first we must select it. Select the **Magic Wand** ( 🪄 ) tool.

6. In the **Options** bar, set the tolerance to **20** and make sure **contiguous** is checked.

7. Click on the **black** background around Riddick.

8. **Shift–Click** on any areas of black background that were not selected to add them to the selection. Don't forget to click between the ropes!

9. If some of the selection cuts into Riddick's body you can do **one** of the following:

   A. Subtract it using the **Lasso** ( 🔾 ) tool while holding the **Option** key (MAC) or the **Alt** key (WINDOWS).

   B. Switch into **Quick Mask Mode** ( ▣ ):

   – Double-click the **Quick Mask Mode** ( ▣ ) button and make sure Color Indicates: **Selected Areas.** Click **OK.**

   – Use the **Brush** ( ✏ ) tool to paint white over any shaded areas of Riddick's body.

   – When done with the selection, switch back to **Standard Mode** ( ▣ ).

10. With the selection complete, select the **Eyedropper** ( ✏ ) tool.

11. To sample some of the dark background color near Riddick's head, click once on the image.

12. To fill the selected area with the sampled foreground color you can either:

    – Go into **Edit > Fill** and choose **Foreground Color.** Then click **OK.**

    – Or just hit **Option–Delete** (MAC) or **Alt–Delete** (WINDOWS).

13. To deselect, press **Cmd–D** (MAC) or **Ctrl–D** (WINDOWS).

---

### ADDING MORE BLANK AREA TO THE RIGHT SIDE

1. Go to **Image > Canvas Size** and set the following:
   – Set the width measurement to **percent,** and enter **200**
   – Leave the height as it is.
   – Click the **left-middle** arrow in the Anchor box (as shown here).
   – Canvas extension color: **Foreground.**

   Click **OK.**

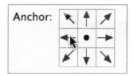

---

### MAKING THE ROPES FADE OUT

1. We want to fade the ropes to the right of Riddick's left leg to black. We'll do this with a gradient, but first we want to create a new layer for it, so go ahead and click the **Create a new layer** ( 🗔 ) button at the bottom of the **Layers** panel.

2. **Double-click** on the new layer's name and type in **rope fade.**

3. Choose the **Gradient** ( ▣ ) tool (you may need to click and hold on the **Paint Bucket** ( 🪣 ) tool to find it).

4. At the left of the **Options** bar, find the gradient preview. As shown below, click the arrow to its right.

5. **Double-click** the **second** thumbnail on the left in the top row, which is the **Foreground to Transparent** gradient. (If you pause a moment over the thumbnail, the name will appear.)

6. Also in the **Options** bar, choose:
   – **Linear gradient** ( ▣ )
   – Mode: **Normal**
   – Opacity: **100%**
   – **Dither** and **Transparency** should be checked.

7. With the **Gradient** ( ▣ ) tool, click and drag from the right edge of the ropes to the left edge (stop before you reach Riddick's shorts), along the angle of the ropes.

## ( CREATING A CUSTOM PATTERN FOR HIS SHORTS )

Now let's make a pattern to place on Riddick's shorts.

1. Go to the **Layers** panel and click on the Background layer to select it.

2. Using the **Rectangular Marquee** ( ▣ ) tool, draw a marquee around both gloves.

3. **Copy** the gloves **(Cmd–C (MAC) or Ctrl–C (WINDOWS)).**

4. Go to **File > New.**

5. In the dialog that opens, under Background Contents, choose **Transparent,** then click **OK.**

6. **Paste** the selection (**Cmd–V (MAC) or Ctrl–V (WINDOWS)**).

7. Choose the **Quick Selection** ( ▨ ) tool. If you can't find it, click and hold on the **Magic Wand** ( ▨ ) tool and then select it.

8. The Quick Selection tool will work like the magic wand, but allows you to paint a selection by clicking and dragging. In the **Options** bar at the top of the screen, pick a medium-sized (about **25 px**), hard-edged brush.

9. To select the glove, start in the center of the right glove and click and drag. Keep dragging around until the entire glove is selected.

10. If you've accidentally selected anything additional, hold **Option (MAC)** or **Alt (WINDOWS)** and click and drag on the parts you want to deselect.

11. Click and drag inside the left glove to select it too.

12. In the Toolbox, click the **Default Colors** ( ) icon to make sure the Foreground color is pure black and the Background color is pure white.

13. To clean up the selection we'll use Quick Mask Mode. At the bottom of the Toolbox, **double-click** the **Quick Mask Mode** ( ) button.

14. In the dialog that appears:

   – Make sure Color Indicates: **Selected Areas.**
   – Under **Color,** make sure the color swatch is a bright color like red or green. If not, click on the color swatch and choose a bright color that will stand out against the image.

15. Click **OK** to close the Quick Mask Options.

16. Use the **Brush** ( ) tool to paint **black** over any missed areas of the gloves you want selected, and press **X** to switch to **white** and paint over to deselect any areas.

17. When done with the selection, in the Toolbox, click on **Edit in Standard Mode** ( ).

18. Go to **Select > Inverse.**

19. Press **Delete** (MAC) or **Backspace** (WINDOWS).

20. Press **Cmd–D** (MAC) or **Ctrl–D** (WINDOWS) to deselect.

21. Go to **Edit > Free Transform.**

22. The Scale options now appear in the **Options** bar at the top of the screen. In the Scale area, click the **Maintain Aspect Ratio** ( ) button between the Width and Height values to keep it from distorting the image.

23. For Width, enter a value of **20%.** Then click the checkbox ( ) at the right of the Options bar (or press **Enter** or **Return**).

24. With the **Rectangular Marquee** ( ) tool, draw a box around the gloves that is a little bigger than the gloves.

25. Go to **Edit > Define Pattern.**

26. Name it **yourname-boxing gloves** and click **OK.**

27. We'll leave this file open just in case we need it later, but now switch back to the **Riddick Bowe** file. If you can't see it, go into the **Window** menu and at the bottom choose **Riddick Bowe.**

### FILLING THE SHORTS WITH A PATTERN

Riddick's shorts are a little boring, so let's add that boxing glove pattern.

1. In the **Layers** panel, make sure the **Background** layer is still selected.

2. Choose the **Magic Wand** ( ) tool and set the tolerance to **50.**

3. Click somewhere on the light part of Riddick's shorts.

4. **Shift–click** on a few other light areas of the shorts to add them to the selection. Ignore the darker wrinkles for now.

5. In the Toolbox, click the **Edit in Quick Mask Mode** ( ▣ ) button.

6. Choose the **Brush** ( ✎ ) tool.

7. In the **Options** bar, set the **Opacity** and **Flow** to **100%.**

8. Pick a medium-sized, hard-edged brush.

9. You'll want shading across the entire surface of Riddick's shorts, so use **black** to add shading over the missing wrinkles, sections of the waistband, and any other missing areas. Paint over the words on the trunks, too.

10. If areas outside the shorts (such as the ropes) are selected, type **X** on the keyboard to swap the Foreground and Background colors. Now paint **white** over any shaded areas outside those shorts.

11. In the Toolbox, click the **Edit in Standard Mode** ( ▣ ) button.

12. In the **Layers** panel, click the **New Fill or Adjustment Layer** ( ◑ ) button and choose **Pattern.**

13. Your boxing gloves pattern should already be selected, so click **OK.** If it wasn't selected, click the pattern thumbnail and choose it.

14. The shorts look very flat right now, but Blending Modes can change the way in which the pattern blends with the shorts. At the top of the **Layers** panel, change the Mode from **Normal** to **Multiply.**

    With the **Multiply** blending mode, this layer can only darken the image behind it, so the dark areas of the shorts on the background layer show through. Feel free to experiment with other blending modes to compare the results.

15. The gloves are still a little bright. At the top of the **Layers** panel, next to the Blend Mode, change the **Opacity** to **60%.**

16. If you decide you'd like to reposition the pattern within the shorts, go to the **Layers** panel and **double-click** the layer's thumbnail ( ▣ ).

    With the **Pattern Fill** dialog box open, click and drag on the main image to move the pattern. Click **OK** when you're done.

17. Congratulations—Riddick would be proud!
    Save this as a Photoshop document if you wish.

## EXERCISE OVERVIEW

The standard print image is CMYK and has a resolution of 300 ppi (pixels per inch). However, digital cameras capture images as RGB at 72 ppi or slightly higher. We will modify an image that was taken with a digital camera, and properly prepare it for print.

1. From the **Photoshop Class** folder, open the file **koala.jpg.**

2. Go to **Image > Mode > CMYK Color.** If you get a message, click OK.

3. Go to **Image > Image Size.** Do NOT click OK until we say!

4. Notice that the **Resolution** for this file is **72** but the **Document Size** is **32.444** by **48.667** inches. This means you'd get a large print, but low quality.

5. At the bottom, uncheck **Resample Image.**

6. For Resolution, type **300.**

7. Notice the **Document Size** reduces to **7.787** by **11.68** inches. This means you'd get a smaller print, but high quality.

   This is the largest size you can print the photo at "full" quality. It was important to uncheck **Resample Image** before doing this. Resampling means to add, remove or recalculate pixels. We do **not** want to add or remove pixels. Instead we are shrinking the pixels in the printout. At 300 pixels per inch, pixels are too small to be seen. Refer to the diagram on the next page for an illustration of this.

8. Click **OK.**

9. Go to **File > Save As.**

10. Use the instructions below to save this image as a **Photoshop Document (.psd)** or **TIFF.** What's the difference? There is virtually no difference for this image. However, TIFFs are more widely accepted in non-Adobe programs, and often have slightly smaller file sizes if LZW compressed. Either choice will maintain full image quality.

| **TO SAVE AS A PSD** | **TO SAVE AS A TIFF** |
|---|---|
| 1. Under **Format,** choose **Photoshop.** | 1. Under **Format,** choose **TIFF.** |
| 2. Name it **yourname-koala.psd.** | 2. Name it **yourname-koala.tif.** |
| 3. Click **Save.** If asked to maximize compatibility, leave it checked on and click **OK.** | 3. Click **Save.** |
| 4. **Close** the file. | 4. Under Image Compression, choose **LZW.** LZW compression is a lossless compression that decreases file size, while maintaining full image quality. Though widely accepted, some applications may not be able to use LZW-compressed TIFFs. |
| | 5. Click **OK.** |
| | 6. **Close** the file. |

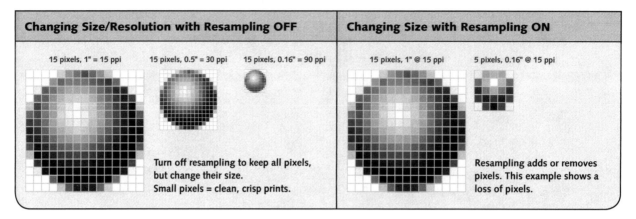

**Changing Size/Resolution with Resampling OFF**

15 pixels, 1" = 15 ppi    15 pixels, 0.5" = 30 ppi    15 pixels, 0.16" = 90 ppi

Turn off resampling to keep all pixels, but change their size.
Small pixels = clean, crisp prints.

**Changing Size with Resampling ON**

15 pixels, 1" @ 15 ppi    5 pixels, 0.16" @ 15 ppi

Resampling adds or removes pixels. This example shows a loss of pixels.

## EXERCISE PREVIEW

## EXERCISE OVERVIEW

Many times, the same content will be used for both print and web, and needs to be converted appropriately. Web images use RGB color and a resolution of 72 ppi, which corresponds to the number of pixels per inch that monitors display. Also, when you're saving images for the web, file size becomes an important issue. Larger files take longer to download!

1. From the **Photoshop Class** folder, open the file **opera house.tif.**

2. Before making this web-ready, it's a good practice to save a copy.
   **Go to File > Save As.**

3. Under format, choose **Photoshop.**

4. Name it **yourname-opera house-web.psd**
   Now if changes are needed further on, there will be a clean original copy that can be used to re-save for web.

5. Go to **Image > Mode > RGB Color.**

6. Go to **Image > Image Size.**

7. Notice that the **Resolution** is 300. We need something less for the web.

8. At the bottom, check on **Resample Image.**

9. From the **Resample Image** menu, choose **Bicubic Automatic.**

   Behind the scenes Photoshop CS6 will automatically choose **Bicubic Sharper** because we'll be reducing the image's size. **Bicubic Sharper** helps maintain a bit more sharpness than **Bicubic.** Prior to CS6 we had to manually **Bicubic Sharper** each time, so CS6's **Bicubic Automatic** is nice because it does it for us!

> ### RESAMPLING
>
> **Resampling** means to **add/remove/recalculate** pixels.
>
> When **Resample Image** is **checked,** the number of pixels actually changes. Either pixels are removed, creating an image with less pixel information, or pixels are added—these "made-up" pixels often result in a less detailed, more blurry image.
>
> When it is **unchecked,** resizing or changing the resolution of the image will not affect the number of pixels in the image—but you can convert a large printing, low resolution image to a smaller printing, high resolution version, or vice versa.

**10.** Under Resolution, type **72.**

Notice the number of pixels have been reduced. We don't need all of them so resampling will throw out/recalculate the reduced number of pixels we need.

**11.** Make sure **Constrain Proportions** is checked.

**12.** Under Pixel Dimensions: Width, enter **400.** The height will change automatically to maintain the proportions of the image. (Currently, the average screen size of most web surfers is 1024 pixels wide by 768 pixels tall.)

**13.** Click **OK.**

**14.** Go to **File > Save for Web.**

**15.** A new window appears, allowing you to adjust compression settings and preview the final image. Click the **4-Up** tab at the top.

**16.** You're now looking at the original, uncompressed image in the upper left of the window, and three compressed versions, each using a different setting. Click on the **upper right** image.

**17.** In the settings on the right, from the menu **below** the **Preset** menu, choose **JPEG.**

NOTE: The JPEG format is best for photos. It maintains good quality at a small file size. Be careful, though—the more you compress JPEGs, the more they will degrade and visual distortions will appear.

**18.** For the **Quality** setting on the right side of the window, type **100.**

Note that the file size appears under each of the compressed preview images. While this doesn't cause much visual distortion, we can get a much smaller file if we try a lower quality.

**19.** Click on the **lower left** image. Choose **JPEG** and set the Quality to **0.**

This is too distorted for most purposes, but the file size is small!

**20.** Click on the **lower right** image. Choose **JPEG** and set the Quality to **70.**

This is getting closer. There's only minor distortion. The trade-off between quality and file size reaches a good balance here.

**21.** Notice that there's a thicker border around the **lower right** image preview area. That indicates it's the selected version. Click **Save** to save a copy of this one.

**22.** Make sure it's named **yourname-opera-house-web.jpg.**

NOTE: When naming files for the web, DO NOT use spaces in the filename. Spaces will cause problems with web browsers. Use dashes or underscores instead. Photoshop will automatically replace any spaces with dashes.

23. Navigate to the **Photoshop Class** folder and click **Save** (Image Only).

24. You should now be looking at the original Photoshop file. Go to **File > Save.** This will save the JPEG quality settings. So if changes need to be made later, it will remember the Save for Web settings we used for this specific file!

25. **Close** the file.

**EXERCISE PREVIEW**

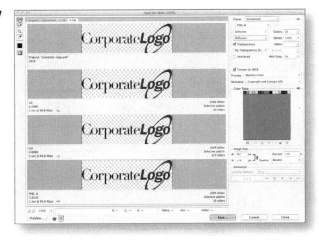

**EXERCISE OVERVIEW**

Photographs and images with many colors optimize better as JPEGs, but files
with few colors (or areas of flat solid color) are ideal for GIF or PNG compression.

1. From the **Photoshop Class** folder, open the file **corporate-logo.psd**.

2. Although this image is already in **RGB** mode at **72 ppi,** we should crop out the empty
   pixels to make the file size smaller. We could use the **Crop** ( ) tool and trim it
   manually, but there's a better way. Go to **Image > Trim** and set the following:

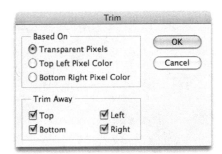

   Click **OK,** and Photoshop quickly and precisely trims the image for you!

3. Go to **File > Save for Web.**

4. In the settings on the right, from the menu **below** the **Preset** menu, choose **GIF.**

   The GIF format shrinks file size by reducing the total number of colors in an image.
   GIFs may have up to 256 colors, but generally you'll need far fewer than that.

5. From the **Colors** setting on the right, choose **16** colors.

6. From the menu to the left of **Colors,** choose the **Selective** color palette.

   **Adaptive, Selective** and **Perceptual** base their color choices on the actual image.
   The other options are preset color palettes, and therefore are typically not
   desirable. We chose Selective in this case because it was the smallest file size,
   and visually there was almost no difference between the three options.

7. The **Dither** option uses scattered pixels to represent intermediate colors, and often makes gradual blends look smoother. We don't need that in this image, so in the menu immediately below **Selective,** choose **No Dither.**

8. From the **Matte** menu, choose whatever color you'd want to use as the background of your imaginary website (in this case white).

   GIF transparency does not allow for partial transparency. Therefore any partially transparent pixels must become opaque. The Matte color is used as a background blend color for any pixels that are partially transparent in the original image. Choosing a color similar to your background allows the edges to better blend with the background of the webpage it will be used on.

9. Make sure that the **Transparency** checkbox is checked.

10. Choose the **Zoom** ( 🔍 ) tool on the left side of the window.

11. Click on the image to zoom in. You'll find that the formerly translucent pixels around the edge of the logo are blended with the **Matte** color to form completely opaque pixels.

### COMPARING GIF TO PNG-8

GIF and PNG-8 compressions work almost exactly the same, but PNG is newer. PNG files are often smaller than GIFs but not always. Since all the settings are the same, we can do a quick test right now to see which is better for this graphic.

1. Take note of the GIF's current file size.

2. In the settings on the right, from the menu **below** the **Preset,** change **GIF** to **PNG-8.**

3. Notice how the PNG is smaller? In our experience, a PNG with the same settings as a GIF is typically 5–25% smaller. For regular text, GIF is sometimes smaller, so you should typically do a test and go with whichever format yields a smaller file size.

4. Click **Save** and save it as **yourname-logo.png** into the **Photoshop Class** folder.

   NOTE: You may have heard bad things about web browser support for PNGs. The problems weren't with the PNG-8 we used in this exercise. PNG-8 works great in all browsers. The problem you may have heard was a lack of support for PNG-24's alpha (partial) transparency. Alpha transparency now works in all the latest browsers (IE, Firefox and Safari). But Internet Explorer only started to support PNG-24's alpha transparency in IE 7. IE 6 and earlier displayed gray instead of the semi-transparency.

   For more information about color palettes, GIF, PNG and JPEG formats, check the reference section in the back of this workbook.

## EXERCISE PREVIEW

BEFORE          AFTER

## EXERCISE OVERVIEW

What a horribly washed out image! We are going to make some color adjustments, but this time we'll use Adjustment Layers to gain more flexibility for future editing.

NOTE: The screenshots on this page show Photoshop's lighter interface. Most of the screenshots in this book depict Photoshop's default darker interface. Throughout this book we may use the lighter interface when it improves the print quality. (Interface brightness can be changed by going into the **Photoshop** menu (MAC) or **Edit** menu (WINDOWS) and choosing **Preferences > Interface** and clicking on the desired **Color Theme**.)

1. From the **Photoshop Class** folder, open the file **na pali coast.tif.**

2. Go to **View > Fit on Screen (Cmd–0** (MAC) **or Ctrl–0** (WINDOWS)**).**

3. Let's start by properly setting our white and black points, and adjusting the contrast. At the bottom of the **Layers** panel, click on **Create new fill or adjustment layer (** 🔘 **), and from the menu, choose **Curves.**

4. You will see the curves open in the **Properties** panel, as shown to the right. You may need to resize the window to see all these options.

5. Now we are ready to do some color correction. Look at the histogram and notice in the bottom left corner that it has no peaks. This means there are no pixels that are black or very dark gray.

6. As shown below, to fix this, hold **Option** (MAC) or **Alt** (WINDOWS) while you drag the **Black** point ( 🔺 ) slider to the right.

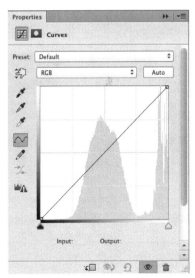

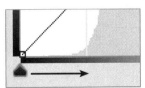

The image will turn white, but as you get close to the beginning of the histogram's "hill" some small pixels will start to appear in various colors. When you see a few of the colored pixels appear, stop dragging. Those pixels have now been set to black.

**7.** The photo looks a little cool and bluish. At the top of the **Properties** panel, where it now says **RGB**, choose **Blue** as shown below.

**8.** Click in the center of the curve and **drag down** a bit. That takes out some of the blue.

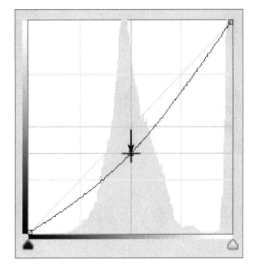

**9.** In the **Layers** panel, **double-click** on **Curves 1** and rename it **contrast & color.**

**10.** The sky is still too bright, but the rest looks good. At the bottom of the **Layers** panel, click on **Create new fill or adjustment layer** ( ⬛ ) and choose **Curves.**

**11.** Looking at just the sky for reference, make the following adjustment:

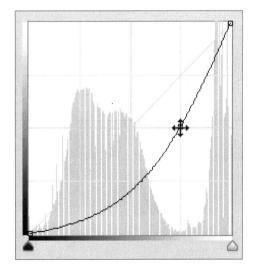

Make sure the sky looks good, and don't worry about the land. We'll be hiding (masking out) any unwanted areas in a moment.

12. In the **Layers** panel, **double-click** Curves 1 and rename it **sky.**

## MASKING OUT THE ADJUSTMENTS

1. In the **sky** layer, click the **layer mask thumbnail** so it is highlighted, as shown to the right. You will see that it is highlighted when brackets appear around the empty white box. We are going to edit this layer mask.

2. Choose the **Gradient** (  ) tool.

3. At the left of the **Options** bar, click the arrow ( ) next to the gradient preview to open the gradient panel, and **double-click** the **third** thumbnail on the left in the top row, which is the **Black, White** gradient.

4. Also in the **Options** bar, choose:
   – **Linear gradient** ( )
   – Mode: **Normal**
   – Opacity: **100%**
   – **Dither** and **Transparency** should be checked.

5. Starting one third of the way up from the bottom (around the brown dirt), drag **up** to the top of the mountain range.

6. The black on the mask has hidden the darkening effect of this adjustment layer at the bottom, and the mask's white has made it visible at the top. There may be parts we want to darken or lighten. Choose the **Brush** ( ) tool.

7. In the Toolbox, click the **Default colors** ( ) icon.

8. In the **Options** bar, choose a huge brush (at least **250 px**) with **0% hardness.**

9. Also in the **Options** bar, lower the **Opacity** to **20%.**

10. Painting white with a 20% Opacity on the mask will slowly reveal the darker **sky** curves adjustment. Paint anywhere that looks a little bright to darken it a bit.

11. Likewise, press **X** to swap the Foreground/Background colors so you have **Black.** Now paint anywhere that looks a bit too dark to mask that layer and brighten it up.

## MAKE THOSE COLORS POP

This photo is still a little dull. We want that Hawaiian foliage to really pop out!

1. At the bottom of the **Layers** panel, click on **Create new fill or adjustment layer** ( ), and from the menu, choose **Hue/Saturation.**

2. In the **Properties** panel, move the Saturation slider to the right to somewhere between **10–20.** Experiment with what you think looks best. We want to add color, but not make it look fake.

3. We'd like to compare the final image to the original. A nice way to do this (and keep the file organized) is to put the layers into a Layer Group. In the **Layers** panel, make sure the top layer is still selected.

4. Hold **Shift** and click on the **contrast & color** layer.
   All three adjustment layers should now be selected.

5. Go into **Layer > Group Layers (Cmd–G ⬭MAC⬭ or Ctrl–G ⬭WINDOWS⬭).**

6. In the **Layers** panel, you should now see a folder. **Double-click** the folder's name and change the name to **my adjustments.**

7. Click the **arrow** ( ▶ ) to the left of the **my adjustments** layer group to expand it and see your layers are inside.

8. Click the **eye** ( 👁 ) beside **my adjustments** layer group a few times to hide and show all the layers it contains. This lets you see a before and after. Pow!

   When you see the background layer without the effect of the adjustment layers, it's clear that the original layer is *unchanged.* Adjustment layers allow flexibility of editing, and they preserve the original image!

9. **File > Save As** as **yourname-na pali coast.psd,** setting **Format** to **Photoshop** to maintain layer editability.

**EXERCISE PREVIEW**

**EXERCISE OVERVIEW**

We'll use a Layer Mask to remove the background from around the hat.
Layer Masks offer the most editing flexibility and they are non-destructive.

### SELECTING THE HAT

1. From the **Photoshop Class** folder, open the image **hat.tif.**

2. Choose the **Magnetic Lasso** ( ) tool.

3. In the **Options** bar, make sure it has the following settings:
   – Feather: **0 px**
   – Width: **10 px**
   – Contrast: **10%**
   – Frequency: **57**

4. Click **once** along the brim to start the lasso selection.
   Do not click and hold. Just click once.

5. Move the cursor along the edges of the hat, and the lasso will lay down points
   along the path as the cursor moves. Keep in mind the following tips:
   • When you reach a corner or tricky place, click to manually place a point.
   • Press **Delete** (MAC) or **Backspace** (WINDOWS) to back up and delete points that have
     been placed incorrectly.

6. When you reach the end, place the cursor over the first point, so it changes to
   a , and click to finish the selection.

7. In the Options bar, click the **Refine Edge** button.

8. At the top of the window, click on the thumbnail image next to **View:** and
   choose **On Black.**

9. Enter the following settings:
   – Radius: **0 px**
   – Smooth: **10**
   – Feather: **0.5 px**
   – Contrast: **0 %**
   – Shift Edge: **Around –40**, but experiment with what looks best for you.

   Click **OK.**

10. In the **Layers** panel, **double-click** the **Background** layer and name it **hat.**
    We do this because **Background** layers cannot be transparent or have layer
    masks. We just turned it into a normal layer so we can add the layer mask.

11. At the bottom of the **Layers** panel, click the **Add Layer Mask ( )** button.

12. At the bottom of the **Layers** panel, click the **Create new fill or
    adjustment layer (  ) button**, and from the menu, choose **Solid Color.**

13. Choose **Black** and click **OK.**

14. In the **Layers** panel, click and drag the **Color Fill** layer below the **hat** layer.

### CLEANING UP THE EDGES

There may be spots showing through from the old background and the brim
edge should be softer. Let's start by fixing the top part of the hat. Later we'll fix
the brim.

1. In the **Layers** panel, **double-click** the **Color Fill** layer's thumbnail (  ).

2. Set the following RGB values:
   R: **0**
   G: **70**
   B: **100**

   Click **OK.**

3. In the **Layers** panel, click the **hat** layer mask (  ).

4. Select the **Brush** (  ) tool.

5. In the **Options** bar, choose a **small-sized, fairly-hard** brush. We recommend
   about **8 px diameter** and **90% hardness.** This size will let you get into the
   corners nicely.

   Make sure **Opacity** and **Flow** are set to **100%.**

6. Press **D** to set default white and black foreground and background colors.

7. Press the **X** key to switch the foreground/background colors so the foreground
   color is **black.**

8. Paint over areas where you see the original light background color around the
   hat. This will remove it, kind of like you are erasing it.

9. As needed, reduce the brush size to get into corners, etc.

10. If you removed any parts of the hat and want to reveal them, remember:
    • Paint **White** over any parts you want to reveal (like the hat).
    • Paint **Black** over any parts you want to hide (like the background).
    • Press the **X** key to switch the foreground and background colors.

### FINISHING UP

The front and back of the brim are blurry in the photo, but the edge of our mask makes them look crisp.

1. Select the **Blur** ( ) tool.

2. In the **Options** bar, choose a **medium-sized soft brush** (about **40 px, 0% hardness**).

3. Click and drag to blur the edges of the brim in the front and back.

4. In the **Layers** panel, select the **Color Fill** layer.

5. Drag it to the **Trash** ( ) button to delete it. Now you should be left with a transparent checkerboard background.

   To save this file, we need to choose a file format appropriate for the layout program you use. Continue with the InDesign section below.

### IMPORTING THE IMAGE INTO INDESIGN

1. Go to **File > Save As.**

2. Navigate to the **Kissimmee Brochure** folder.

3. Set **Format** to **Photoshop** and name the image **yourname-hat.psd**. Click **Save.**
   NOTE: TIFF can also work, but you must check on **Save Transparency.**

4. Launch **InDesign.**

5. From the **Kissimmee Brochure** folder, open the InDesign file **Brochure-add hat.indd.**

6. Choose the **Selection** ( ) tool.

7. On the bottom left, click on the empty rectangular picture box.

8. Go to **File > Place.**

9. Choose **yourname-hat.psd** and click **Open.**

10. Go to **View > Display Performance > High Quality Display.**

11. Zoom in and examine the blurry, semi-transparent parts. Very nice.

    Enjoy your work—you're done! Because we no longer need this file, close the InDesign file and do NOT save changes.

### STRAIGHT LINES

*Using the Pen Tool*
*Adjusting the Workspace*
*Arranging Objects*
*Color Fills*

### CURVES

*Drawing Curves (Pen Tool)*
*Anchor Points and Direction Points*
*Default Fill and Stroke*

### CORNERS AND CURVES

*Drawing Corners and Curves (Pen Tool)*
*Adjusting Anchor Points*

### NO SMOKING SIGN

*Fill and Stroke*
*Basic Shape Tools*
*Grouping Objects*
*Layers Panel*
*Working with Templates*
*Saving Illustrator Files: Options*


*Continued…*

# Illustrator Topics
## SECTION C

### SUPER HERO

*Live Trace and Live Paint*
*Tracing Hand-Drawn Images*
*Coloring Live Paint Objects*
*Brushes*
*Flare Tool*

### JUGGLING COLORS AND GRADIENTS

*Dashed Lines and Stroke Options*
*Saving Colors as Swatches*
*Blending Modes*
*Gradient Tool*
*Saving Gradient Swatches*

### COMBINING SHAPES WITH THE PATHFINDER

*Merging Paths (Pathfinder)*
*Transparency Options*
*Grouping Objects*

**EXERCISE PREVIEW**

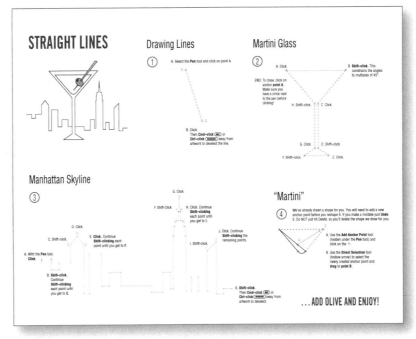

**EXERCISE OVERVIEW**

The **Pen** ( ) tool is the heart of Illustrator. This exercise gets you started drawing simple lines and shapes.

1. Go to **File > Open**. Navigate to the **Desktop**, then into the **Class files** folder, then into the **Illustrator Class** folder. (All files for the class are located in this **Illustrator Class** folder). Open the file **Straight Lines Template.ai**

2. Do a **File > Save As**.

   At the bottom, make sure **Format** is set to **Adobe Illustrator (ai)** document. Navigate into the same **Illustrator Class** folder you opened it from. Name the file **yourname-Straight Lines.ai**

   Click **Save**. In the dialog that appears, leave the default options checked and click **OK**.

**GETTING SET UP & USING THE TEMPLATE**

1. As shown below, toward the bottom of the Toolbox, click on the **Default Fill and Stroke** ( ) button. This makes your fill white and the stroke black.

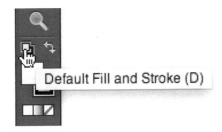

2. As shown to the right, click the **Fill Icon** to make it active.

3. Click the **None** ( ) button just below that.

4. Follow the on-screen directions in the file. When you have completed the directions, save your changes and move on to the next steps below.

Fill (X)

### ( FINISHING UP ONCE YOU'RE DONE WITH THE TEMPLATE )

You've drawn all the shapes for the Manhattan Martini image, so let's arrange them.

1. Using the **Selection** ( ) tool, click on the **Glass** you drew.

2. **Shift–click** the "**Martini**" and the Manhattan Skyline shape.

3. Now that all three shapes are selected **Copy** them **(Edit > Copy).**

4. Go to **File > Open** and from the **Illustrator Class** folder, choose **Manhattan Martini.ai**

5. **Paste** your objects **(Edit > Paste).**

6. We've included the **Olive** and **Toothpick** for you. You'll learn how to draw curved lines in an upcoming exercise, but we've provided these shapes for now.

7. **Click away** from the artwork to deselect it.

8. Let's arrange things starting with the **Glass.** With the **Selection** ( ) tool, click on it and drag it to the **center** of the page.

### ( COLORING THE MARTINI GLASS )

1. This shape needs a **white** fill. With the **Glass** still selected, go to the Toolbox and click the **Fill Icon.**

2. Go to the **Color** panel (**Window > Color** opens it if you don't see it).

3. Choose **White** by clicking on the white swatch at the top left of the color bar.

4. Click on the **"Martini"** shape and place it inside the glass... and while it's still selected, choose **Object > Arrange > Bring to Front.**

5. A light blue color would look good for the "Martini," so go to the **Color** panel.

6. If the **Color** panel is only displaying a color bar (not color sliders), go into the **panel menu** ( ) at the top right of the panel and choose **Show Options.**

7. If the **Color** panel isn't showing **CMYK** color sliders, go into the **panel menu** ( ) at the top right of the panel and choose **CMYK.**

8. The first line is **C** (**C** stands for **C**yan). Type **7** in the box at the end of this line and press **Return** (MAC) or **Enter** (WINDOWS). If the other 3 colors, **MYK**, don't all become **0**, then make them **0**.

## ARRANGING THE OTHER ELEMENTS

1. Click on the **Manhattan Skyline** and place it behind the glass.

2. Notice that the line of the Skyline is on top of the glass. With the Skyline still selected, choose **Object > Arrange > Send To Back.**

3. The Skyline is too big compared to the glass. With the shape still selected, **double-click** the **Scale** ( ) tool in the Toolbox.

4. In the dialog box that appears, for **Uniform** Scale, enter **75%** and click **OK.**

5. Reposition the Skyline if needed. Make sure to choose the **Selection** ( ) tool.

6. The three shapes making up the **Olive and toothpick** are in the **top right** corner of your screen.

7. Stay in that corner and assemble the shapes using the **Selection** ( ) tool so the toothpick is touching/poking through the olive.

8. Select all three shapes and go to **Object > Group.**

9. With the olive and pick still selected, choose **Object > Arrange > Bring to Front.**

10. Move the olive and pick onto the Martini Glass.

11. Do a **File > Save As** and name it **yourname-Manhattan Martini.ai**

12. In the dialog that appears, leave the default options checked and click **OK.**

---

### SAVING ILLUSTRATOR FILES

Once you click the **Save** button, an Options dialog will appear. You should keep the **Version** set to the version of Illustrator you are currently using (in our case that's **Illustrator CS6**).

If you will need to edit the file with an older version of Illustrator, you can save to an older version, but be careful! Type will potentially be changed when saving to a Legacy Version (a non CS version). Hidden Appearance attributes will be lost in any format before CS4. New features such as effects, transparency, nested layers, etc. will be changed when saving to versions earlier than Illustrator 9, while things like symbols were new to Illustrator 10.

**Create PDF Compatible File** should be checked on to ensure the best compatibility with other Creative Suite applications such as InDesign and Photoshop.

**Embed ICC Profiles** is an advanced topic since it relates to a color managed workflow. For now, don't worry about it and just stick with whatever your default is (on or off).

**Use Compression** should be checked on to reduce file size (without loss of quality).

**EXERCISE PREVIEW**

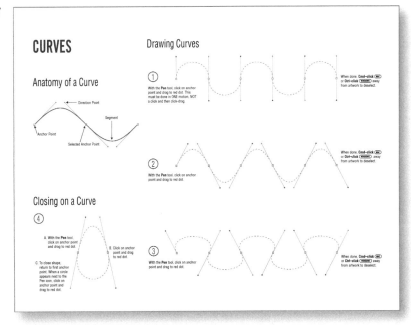

**EXERCISE OVERVIEW**

Continuing in our quest for mastery of the **Pen** ( ) tool, this exercise walks you through creating curved lines and shapes.

1. From the **Illustrator Class** folder, open the file **Curves Template.ai**

2. Do a **File > Save As,** naming the file **yourname-Curves.ai**

3. Click **Save.** In the dialog that appears, leave the default options checked and click **OK.**

4. In the Toolbox, click on the **Default Fill and Stroke** ( ) button.

5. In the Toolbox, click on the **Fill Icon** and then click the **None** ( ) button.

6. Follow the on-screen directions in the file. When you have completed the directions, **File > Save** your changes.

**EXERCISE PREVIEW**

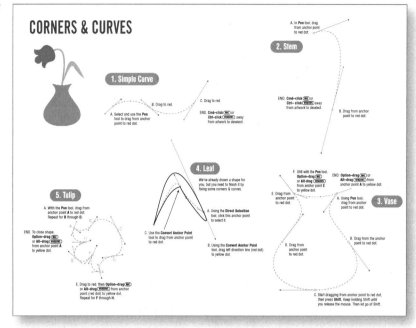

## EXERCISE OVERVIEW

Corners can be tricky to draw, but this template walks you through drawing them and makes it quite easy.

1.  From the **Illustrator Class** folder, open the file **Corners & Curves Template.ai**

2.  Do a **File > Save As,** naming the file **yourname-Corners & Curves.ai**

3.  Click **Save.** In the dialog that appears, leave the default options checked and click **OK.**

### GETTING SET UP & USING THE TEMPLATE

1.  In the Toolbox, click on the **Default Fill and Stroke** ( ) button.

2.  In the Toolbox, click on the **Fill Icon** and then click the **None** ( ) button.

3.  Follow the on-screen directions in the file. When you have completed the directions, save your changes and move on to the next section here in the workbook.

### FINISHING UP ONCE YOU'RE DONE WITH THE TEMPLATE

You've drawn the shapes that make up the complete image so let's put them all together.

1.  If you closed the **yourname-Corners & Curves.ai** file, please open it again.

2.  Using the **Selection** ( ) tool, click on the **Stem** you drew.

3. **Shift–click** the **Vase, Leaf** and **Tulip** so they are also selected.

4. Now that all four shapes are selected, **Copy** them **(Edit > Copy).**

5. Create a new file **(File > New)** with the following options:

   – Profile: **Print**
   – Orientation: **Portrait** (  ) (that's an upright, tall page)

   Click **OK.**

6. Do a **File > Save As,** naming the file **yourname-flowers.ai**

7. Click **Save,** and in the dialog that appears, click **OK.**

8. Now **Paste** your objects **(Edit > Paste).**

9. **Click away** from the artwork to deselect the shapes.

10. The shapes need to be arranged. Let's start with the **Vase.** Using the **Selection** (  ) tool, drag it to the center of the page.

11. Drag the **Stem** into place above the Vase.

12. Drag the **Tulip** to the end of the Stem.

13. Drag the **Leaf** into place above the Vase and to the right of the Stem.

14. **Click away** from the artwork to deselect the shapes. The composition is now complete, but some color would really enhance this.

15. Click on the **Vase** to select it.

16. Click on the **Fill Icon** (in the Toolbox). Then in the **Color** panel, enter **60** next to **M** (Magenta) and **90** next to **Y** (Yellow). Cyan and blacK should remain at **0.**

    For the rest of this workbook, when we ask you to enter **CMYK** values, we will use a shorthand direction. The above values would be written **60m** and **90y.**

17. Click on the **Tulip** to select it.

18. The **Fill** should still be active, so in the **Color** panel, enter **7c** and **94m.**

    NOTE: When you type in color values, Illustrator will sometimes reinsert the values from the last color you specified into the remaining fields. So for any color values you aren't specifying, be sure to make them **0** if Illustrator didn't.

19. Click on the **Leaf** to select it.

20. The **Fill** should still be active, so in the **Color** panel enter **66c** and **100y.**

21. Click on the **Stem** to select it.
    The Stem and Leaf should both be the same green. The Stem is just a line, so it needs a stroke color, not a fill color.

22. Click on the **Stroke Icon** (in the Toolbox).

**23.** In the **Color** panel, enter **66c** and **100y.**

> NOTE: Once you click in a number field of the **Color** panel, just hit **Tab** to jump to the field below. This makes entering numbers for colors faster!

**24.** With the Stem still selected, in the **Control** panel at the top of the screen, enter a stroke of **5 pt.**

**25.** Let's get rid of those black strokes on everything else.
Choose the **Selection** (  ) tool. Starting outside the shapes, **click and drag** a selection marquee over everything. When you let go, they will be selected.

**26.** **Shift–Click** the **Stem** to deselect it.

**27.** In the **Toolbox,** make sure that the **Stroke Icon** is active and is black. If it is showing question marks, the stem is probably still selected.

**28.** Click the **None** ( ) button.

**29.** Click off the artwork to deselect it.

**30.** Do a **File > Save** and **Close** the file.
Spring has sprung!

### QUESTION MARKS?

When multiple objects are selected, sometimes the Stroke and Fill icons show question marks.

This means that there are multiple Fill or Stroke colors for those objects. Illustrator doesn't know which color to show. If they are all the same color, Illustrator will show that color.

**EXERCISE PREVIEW**

**EXERCISE OVERVIEW**

Here you'll get more practice drawing and creating strokes and fills. You'll learn about the incredibly important and useful Layers panel.

### GETTING STARTED

1. Create a new document **(File > New)** with these settings:

   – Profile: **Print**
   – Orientation: **Portrait** ( ) (that's an upright, tall page)

   Click **OK.**

2. Do a **File > Save As,** naming the document **yourname-No Smoking.ai**

3. Click **Save.** In the dialog that appears, leave the default options checked and click **OK.**

4. Go to **View > Fit Artboard in Window.**

5. Go to **File > Place.**

6. In the **Illustrator Class** folder, click on the **NoSmoking.tif** to select it, and then at the bottom of the window, check **Template.** Next, click **Place.**

7. Make sure you are showing both the **Layers** and **Color** panels. If you cannot see them, go into **Window > Layers** and **Window > Color.**

8. In the **Layers** panel, there are now two layers. The **Template NoSmoking.tif** layer holds the file you placed. You will do the tracing on **Layer 1,** which is already selected as the active layer.

9. Go to **View > Rulers > Show Rulers.**

10. From the top ruler, click and drag down a guide into the center of the circle.

11. From the left ruler, click and drag out another guide into the center of the circle.

12. Go to **View > Guides** and make sure **Lock Guides** is checked.

## DRAWING THE CIRCLE & SLASH LINE

1. Select the **Ellipse** ( ) tool. If you don't see it, click and hold on the **Rectangle** ( ) tool to get it.

2. Hold down **Option–Shift** (MAC) or **Alt–Shift** (WINDOWS), and **click and drag** from the **center point** where the guides meet to the **edges of the circle.**

   NOTE: Holding **Option** (MAC) or **Alt** (WINDOWS) makes the circle draw out from the center point. Holding **Shift** makes the oval a perfect circle.

3. We want to change the stroke to red, so with the circle still selected, click on the **Stroke** Icon in the Toolbox as shown below.

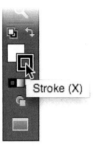

4. In the **Color** panel, make the color **100m, 100y.** (If the Color panel is not displaying CMYK, go into the **panel menu** ( ) at the upper right of the panel and choose CMYK.)

5. With the circle still selected, in the **Stroke** panel **(Window > Stroke),** make the weight **19 pt.**

   NOTE: You can also enter Stroke weight in the **Control** panel at the top of the screen.

6. Right now you are working in **Preview** mode, and you have covered the template by filling the circle. To see the template, go to **View > Outline.**

7. Select the **Line Segment** ( ) tool.

8. Hold down **Option–Shift** (MAC) or **Alt–Shift** (WINDOWS), and **click and drag** from the **center point** to the **edge of the circle,** following the template.

   NOTE: Holding **Shift** constrains the line to a 90° or 45° angle.

9. Keep the line selected and switch back to **Preview** mode. To do this go into the **View** menu and choose **Preview.**

10. The line should already be the proper red color and thickness because it kept the settings you had just used.

11. Go to **Select > Deselect.**

## DRAWING THE CIGARETTE

1.  Before we start to draw the cigarette, we don't want to use the big red stroke we currently have. In the Toolbox click **Default Fill and Stroke** ( ).

2.  Trace over the cigarette using the **Rectangle** ( ) tool for both parts.

3.  You are going to color the cigarette using color swatches. To open the **Swatches** panel go into **Window > Swatches.**

4.  With the **Selection** ( ) tool, select the rectangle that forms the tip of the cigarette.

5.  Click on the **Fill** icon (in the Toolbox) to make sure it's selected.

6.  Give a black fill by clicking on the **black** swatch in the **Swatches** panel.

7.  To change the stroke width, use the **Stroke** panel. For weight type **3 pt.**

8.  Select the left part of the cigarette and give it a **3 pt black** stroke.

9.  Switch into **Outline** mode to draw the smoke.

10. Zoom in (using the **Zoom** ( ) tool or **View > Zoom In**) so the smoke fills more of the screen. Just make sure you can still see all of it.

11. Trace the smoke using the **Pen** ( ) tool.

12. Switch back to **Preview** mode so you can see how things are looking.

13. Make sure both smoke paths have a **3 pt black stroke** and **no** ( ) fill.

## PUTTING IT ALL TOGETHER

1.  Use the **Selection** ( ) tool to select all parts of the **cigarette,** including the smoke, by **Shift–clicking** or by clicking and dragging a marquee around them.

2.  Group the cigarette parts using **Object > Group.**

3.  Move the cigarette group into the center of the circle.

    Wait! Alas, the cigarette is in front of the sign.
    To fix this, you are now going to paste the cigarette in back of the slash.

4.  **Cut** the cigarette group **(Edit > Cut).**

5.  Select the rotated line, or slash. (You have to click on the actual path in the middle of the big stroke to select it. It may be easier to select it in **Outline** mode.)

6.  Choose **Edit > Paste In Back.**

# 4C
**EXERCISE**

## ADDING A FRAME

1. Switch back to **Outline** mode so you can see the template.

2. Select the **Rounded Rectangle** ( ▢ ) tool (if you don't see it, click and hold on the **Rectangle** ( ▢ ) tool to get to it).

3. Hold down **Option** ⟨MAC⟩ or **Alt** ⟨WINDOWS⟩ and click once in the **center** of the circle. It's important just to click (do NOT **hold down** or **drag** the mouse) to bring up the dialog box for precise drawing.

4. In the dialog that appears enter:
   – Width: **194 pt**
   – Height: **194 pt**
   – Corner Radius: **15 pt**

   Click **OK.**

5. Switch back to **Preview** mode and make sure the rounded square has a **white** fill and **3 pt black** stroke.

6. Since the fill obscures the other objects, with the rounded square selected, choose **Object > Arrange > Send to Back.**

7. It looks pretty good but the template is still showing. To hide it look at the **Layers** panel. Notice the **Template NoSmoking.tif** layer. As shown below, click on the visibility icon to its left to hide it.

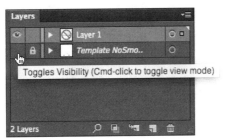

8. Go to **View > Guides > Hide Guides.**

9. Congratulations! You're done. **Save** your changes and print it if you wish.

**EXERCISE PREVIEW**

## EXERCISE OVERVIEW

Often you'll want to take a hand-drawn sketch and convert it into vector graphics so you can edit it in Illustrator. The Image Trace feature makes this very easy to do. After tracing it, you will add color and a background to make the graphic pop.

### TRACING THE SUPERHERO SKETCH

1. In the **Illustrator Class** folder, open the file **super hero.ai**

2. Save as **yourname-the super hero.ai**

3. In the dialog that appears, leave the default options checked and click **OK**.

4. Choose the **Selection** ( ) tool.

5. Go to **File > Place**.

6. Locate **super hero sketch.psd** and click **Place**.

7. Make sure it's still selected, and in the **Control** panel (at the top of the screen) click the **Image Trace** button.

8. The super hero scan has now been traced (converted to vectors) using the default options, but it's missing a lot of details. To customize the quality and settings, towards the left of the **Control** panel (at the top of the screen), click the **Image Trace** ( ) button.

9. In the panel that opens, check on **Preview** (at the bottom).

10. At the top, set the **Preset** to **Sketched Art**.

11. In the **Image Trace** panel, click the triangle to the left of **Advanced** to see more options.

12. Set **Noise** to **1 px.** Notice how many of the lost details have reappeared.

13. Set **Threshold** to **180,** and **Paths** to **90%.**

14. Click the **Trace** button to finish. (If **Trace** is not clickable, this means the Preview function has already updated the changes.)

### ADDING SOME COLOR

1. In the **Control** panel, click the **Expand** button.

2. Go to **Object > Live Paint > Make.** The image won't change at all, but it has been converted to a Live Paint Group, indicated by the starburst bounding box handles ( ⊞ ).

3. **Deselect** the artwork by clicking off of it.

4. Choose the **Live Paint Bucket** ( 🪣 ) tool. If you don't see it, click and hold the **Shape Builder** ( ⬡ ) tool.

5. Notice the color swatches above the bucket cursor. 🖐

6. Press the **Left** and **Right arrow** keys to cycle through the swatches.

7. Put the cursor over the superhero, but DO NOT click yet! Notice that fillable regions are outlined in bright red.

8. Use the arrow keys to choose the proper swatch, then click on an outlined area to fill the superhero. Refer to the guide on the right.

   - Be careful of the black strokes. These are actually fills that can be accidentally filled with another color. If you accidentally change them, just undo it.
   - Don't forget to fill his teeth in with white!
   - Zoom in to fill small areas that are hard to target.

### ADDING A BACKGROUND

1. Go to **File > Place.**

2. In the **Illustrator Class** folder, locate **city sketch.psd** and click **Place.**

3. Choose the **Selection** ( ▶ ) tool.

4. Move the city sketch to the bottom of the document.

5. With the city sketch selected, in the **Image Trace** panel change the **Preset** to **Silhouettes.**

6. Under **Advanced** in the Image Trace panel, uncheck **Ignore White.**

---

### IMAGE TRACE

Once you are done tweaking the options of **Live Trace** and have a nice vector drawing, you can do one of the following:

1. Do nothing, just leave the art in its current live state. This way, the **Image Trace** options can be tweaked later if needed.

2. Click the **Expand** button (in the **Control** panel) to render the vector outlines, so you can manually refine the art using standard tools. After expanding, you cannot tweak the Tracing options.

3. After expanding, use the **Live Paint Bucket** tool to convert it into a Live Paint group.

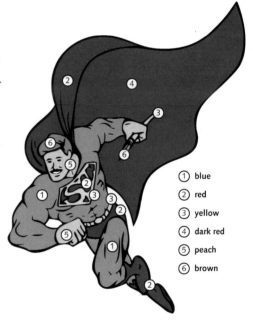

① blue
② red
③ yellow
④ dark red
⑤ peach
⑥ brown

7. In the **Control** panel, click the **Expand** button to turn it into editable artwork.

8. Click off the artwork to deselect it.

9. Choose the **Group Selection** (  ) tool. If you don't see it, click and hold the **Direct Selection** ( ) tool.

10. Select the white sky above the cityscape and press **Delete** to remove it.

11. Choose the **Selection** ( ) tool.

12. Select the cityscape again.

13. Open the **Swatches** panel **(Window > Swatches)**.

14. Make sure that the **fill** icon is active and give it the **dark green** fill.

15. With the city still selected, go to **Object > Arrange > Send to Back**.
    The cityscape does not go behind the starburst because it is on a separate layer.

16. Select the **super hero**.

17. In the Toolbox, **double-click** the **Scale** ( ) tool.

18. Under Uniform, enter a scale of **110%** and Click **OK**.

19. Choose the **Selection** ( ) tool.

20. Position him nicely in the center of the document.

21. Press **Cmd–Shift–A** MAC or **Ctrl–Shift–A** WINDOWS to deselect him.

---

**( FINISHING TOUCHES )**

1. Select the **Paintbrush** ( ) tool.

2. Open the **Brushes** panel **(Window > Brushes)**.

3. In the bottom left corner of the panel, click the **Brush Libraries** ( ) button and from the menu choose **Artistic > Artistic_Calligraphic**.

4. From the panel that opens, select the **5 pt Oval**. If you're unsure which brush it is, go to the **Brush panel menu** ( ) and select **List View** to display all the available brushes listed by name.

5. In the **Color** panel, make sure that the **Stroke** icon is active and change to a **Black** stroke.

6. As shown to the right, use the paintbrush to create a few action lines coming out of the hero's back to make it look like he's flying in to save the day.

7. When finished, close the **Artistic_Calligraphic** brush panel.

8. Choose the **Flare** ( ) tool. If you can't find the flare, click and hold on the **Rounded Rectangle** ( ) tool (or possibly Rectangle tool).

9. At the back of the hero's belt, click and drag out a large solar flare. If you don't like the look of the flare, just undo and try it again.

10. Do a **File > Save** and **Close** the file. Super!

**EXERCISE PREVIEW**

**EXERCISE OVERVIEW**

This poster starts off as a plain grayscale graphic. You'll spice it up by adding colored strokes, fills, and gradients.

### COLORING THE JUGGLER'S BODY

1. In the Illustrator Class folder, open the file **Juggler.ai**

2. This drawing is basically complete, but it needs color. Let's start by hitting the letter **D** on the keyboard to get the default white fill and black stroke.

3. Select the body of the juggler.

4. Give it a **black fill** and a **1 pt black stroke.**

5. Select the diamond pattern on the juggler's legs.

6. Give it a **1 pt stroke** and set the color to **100c** and **39m**
   (and don't forget to set **0y** and **0k** (black).
   NOTE: For this and other color settings, if you don't see CMYK values, go into the **panel menu** ( ⬛ ) and choose **CMYK.**

7. Select the design on the juggler's chest. You will need to click the **sternum** and then **Shift–click** to get the **ribs** too.

8. Make sure the **Fill** swatch is active.

9. In the **Color** panel, make the color **75c, 59y** and set the stroke to **none**.

10. **Shift–click** the sternum to deselect it, so that only the **ribs** are selected.

11. You are now going to reduce the saturation of the color in the ribs.

    Holding down the **Shift** key, slide the cyan portion of the color to approximately **45%.** The yellow will slide with it.

### COLORING THE FLOOR

1. The floor is composed of one background object and a group of diamond floor tiles in front. Select the background by clicking any of the darker areas on the floor.

2. Fill it with **20c, 5m, 5y, 10k.** (You may need to choose CMYK from the panel menu.)

3. Now let's create a new CMYK color swatch, but first, click on the light diamond floor tiles (they're grouped).

4. Change the fill color to **6c, 15y.**

5. Add this new color to the **Swatches** panel. As shown to the right, simply drag the swatch from the **Color** panel over the **Swatches** panel until a highlighted border appears in the **Swatches** panel. When you "drop" the color swatch it will be added to the **Swatches** panel.

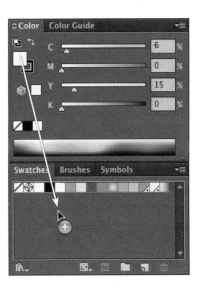

6. **Double-click** on the new swatch to name it **floor tiles**.
   Click **OK**.

7. Select the **shadows** behind, or under, the juggler's legs.

8. Fill them with **10c, 5m, 20k.**

9. Keep the shadows selected and go to the **Transparency** panel **(Window > Transparency).**

10. In the **Transparency** panel you'll see a menu that says **Normal.** Change this to **Multiply.** (This uses the shadow shape to darken the colors that are underneath, thus giving the look of a natural shadow.)

### COLORING THE JUGGLER'S FACE

1. Zoom in and select the outline of the juggler's face.

2. In the **Swatches** panel, make sure the **Find Field** is showing. If it is not, go into the **panel menu** ( ▼≡ ) in the top right corner and choose **Show Find Field.**

3. In the **Find Field,** start typing in **skintone.** Illustrator will select the swatch by showing a white outline around it. Click on this swatch to apply it.

4. **Select > Deselect (Cmd–Shift–A MAC or Ctrl–Shift–A WINDOWS ).**

5. Now you will create your own custom color. In the **Swatches** panel click on the **New Swatch** ( ) button.

   In the **Swatch Options** dialog that opens, enter the following:
   – Name: **Bright Red**
   – Color type: **Process Color, Global** should be checked
   – Color mode: **CMYK**
   – Mix a color that is **100m, 50y.**

   Click **OK.**

6. Apply that color to the lips of the juggler and make sure the stroke is set to **none.**

7. Hit **Cmd–Shift–A** (MAC) or **Ctrl–Shift–A** (WINDOWS) to do a **Select > Deselect.**

8. Now you will create some gradient fills. Go to the **Gradient** panel **(Window > Gradient).**

9. Click on the gradient slider at the bottom to get the color stops ( ) to show.

10. If there are more than 2 color stops ( ), delete the extras by dragging them down and off the panel. Leave color stops ( ) at the beginning and end of the gradient slider so it looks as shown below.

11. **Double-click** the left color stop ( ) in the **Gradient** panel.

12. As shown to the right, click on the **swatches icon** ( ) on the left of the pop-up panel to view the swatches.

13. Select the **dull red** swatch.

14. Click the **color icon** ( ) on the left of the pop-up panel.

15. Change the **tint (T)** of the dull red to **50%.**

16. To close the pop-up panel, press **Escape** (Esc) or click back in the **Gradient** panel.

17. **Double-click** the **right** color stop ( ).

18. Click on the **swatches icon** ( ) on the left, then select the **skintone** swatch.

19. Near the top of the **Gradient** panel, make the Type: **Radial.** (If you don't see this option in the panel, go into the **panel menu** ( ) and choose **Show Options.**)

20. Now that the gradient is done, we want to add it to the **Swatches** panel to save it. At the bottom of the **Swatches** panel, click the **New Swatch** ( 🔲 ) button.

    NOTE: You can also drag and drop the swatch (from the **Gradient** panel) into the Swatch panel to create a swatch.

21. Name the new gradient swatch **cheek.**

22. Drag and drop the swatch onto the circle of the juggler's cheek.

### COLORING THE JUGGLING BALLS

1. Select the top juggling ball.

2. Fill the ball with the **yellow to red** gradient (it's already been created and is in the **Swatches** panel).

3. Make sure the ball is selected, and click on the **Gradient** ( 🔲 ) tool to change the direction of the gradient. With the **Gradient** ( 🔲 ) tool, click on the upper left of the ball and drag to the lower right.

4. Now you will copy this color to the other balls. **Double-click** the **Eyedropper** ( 🖊 ) tool to see its options.

5. At the top, we want **Appearance** to be checked on in BOTH columns. If it's not checked on, do so now. Click **OK.**

6. Use the **Selection** ( ▶ ) tool to select the two lower juggling balls, holding the **Shift** key to get both.

7. With the **Eyedropper** ( 🖊 ) tool, click on your gradient ball to sample its appearance.

8. The other two juggling balls are filled with the gradient. Note that the direction and placement of the gradient stays the same too!

9. Do a **Select > Deselect (Cmd–Shift–A (MAC) or Ctrl–Shift–A (WINDOWS)).**

10. You are now going to edit a gradient. At the top left of the **Gradient** panel, click the arrow ( ▮ ) to bring up a list of all the gradient swatches.

11. Select the **yellow to red** gradient swatch.

12. Click anywhere between the **start** and **end color stops** ( 🔲 ) in the area just below the gradient slider. This will create a new stop ( 🔲 ).

13. Drag the new color stop ( 🔲 ) until the Location number is approximately **80%,** or just type **80%** in the Location field.

14. **Double-click** the new color stop ( 🔲 ).

15. Click the **color icon** ( 🔲 ) on the left and change this color to **74m, 50y.**

16. **Double-click** the last color stop ( 🔲 ) on the right.

**17.** Add to its existing CMYK values **28c.** You've just created a gradient that goes from **yellow** to **red** to a **darker version of the red.**

**18.** To create a new gradient swatch, go to the bottom of the **Swatches** panel and click the **New Swatch** ( ) button.

**19.** In the dialog that appears, name it **juggling balls.**
Click **OK.**

**20.** Drag the new swatch over the juggling balls in the image to change their gradients.

### STYLING THE HAIR AND JUGGLING LINE

**1.** Using the **Selection** ( ) tool, click on a strand of the juggler's hair. (All of the hair should become selected because they are grouped.)

**2.** Zoom in on it so you can see the changes we make.

**3.** Change the hair to have a stroke of **1.5 pt black.**

**4.** In the **Stroke** panel, if the only thing you see is a **Weight** option, go into the **panel menu** ( ) and select **Show Options.**

**5.** Change the cap to **Round Cap** ( ).

**6.** Now select the black line between the juggler's hands.

**7.** Check the **Dashed Line** option in the **Stroke** panel.

**8.** Type **4** above the **first dash** field and **6** above the first gap field. Hit **Return** (MAC) or **Enter** (WINDOWS) to apply it.

**9.** Make sure the **Stroke** icon is active in the Toolbox.

**10.** Select the **bright red** swatch as the stroke color.

**11.** Press **Cmd–Shift–A** (MAC) or **Ctrl–Shift–A** (WINDOWS) to deselect and see the effect.

### COLORING THE BACKGROUND AND TEXT

**1.** Select the box around the juggler.

**2.** Give it a fill of **61c, 30m, 6y, 10k.**

**3.** Give it a **3.5 pt black** stroke.

**4.** Go down to the text underneath the juggler. Select the word MILANO.

**5.** Fill the letters with the gradient **yellow to dk blue** (in the **Swatches** panel).

6. Now use the **Gradient** (  ) tool to play with the direction of the blend. Drag over the type to change the angle and length of the gradient.
   NOTE: You'll notice that at first the gradient blend occurs once in each letter, but if you use the **Gradient** (  ) tool while all the letters are selected, it will sweep the gradient fill across all of the letters at once.

7. Finally, using the **Gradient** (  ) tool, hold **Shift** (to ensure the gradient will be straight up and down) and drag from the **top** of the **M** to the **bottom** of the **M.**

8. Hey, that's pretty nice. **Save** your file as **yourname-juggler.ai** and guess what, you're done!

   NOTE: If you get an alert about spot colors and transparency, just click **Continue.** This is just a warning that converting the file to process colors outside of Illustrator can cause unexpected results. We won't be doing that so it's not a problem.

**EXERCISE PREVIEW**

**EXERCISE OVERVIEW**

The Pathfinder is an excellent way to create shapes and special effects. Instead of drawing the woman by hand, you will take various shapes and cut, overlap, and merge them to create the finished product.

1. From the **Illustrator Class** folder, open the file **geisha.ai**

2. Make sure the **Pathfinder** panel is open (**Window > Pathfinder** if you don't see it).

**CREATING/ASSEMBLING THE ILLUSTRATION**

You will see an assortment of shapes. Many of these shapes have been created by modifying ellipses using the **Direct Selection** ( ) and **Convert Anchor Point** ( ) tools. You'll use the Pathfinder panel to combine them to create more complex shapes that would have been harder to make if you had to draw the final shapes yourself.

1. First we'll create the hairline. With the **Selection** ( ) tool, drag the **Slice Line** over the **Large Oval**. Refer to the example for correct placement.

2. Make sure some of the slice line hangs slightly off the edge of the hair at the bottom.

3. With the line still selected, go to **Object > Path > Divide Objects Below.** This will cut the object into two pieces using the slice line as a guide.

4.  We don't need the smaller piece we've created. Go to **Select > Deselect.**

5.  **Select** and **delete** that slice by-product so you are left with just the shape of the hair.

6.  Move the **hairpiece** over the **face** shape and contemplate a new career in digital hairdressing. Be a good hairdresser though and make sure there are no little white spaces showing through.

7.  **Shift–click** on the face so that both the hair and the face are selected.

8.  In the **Pathfinder** panel, under Pathfinders: click the **Trim** ( ) button. This makes the face into a shape that doesn't include the part obscured by the hair.

9.  The objects are now grouped, but we don't need them to be, so choose **Object > Ungroup.**

10. Select the piece labeled **Hair Bun** and drag it over the hair as shown in the example.

11. Hold **Shift** and **Click** on the hair to add it to your selection (you should have both black objects selected).

12. In the **Pathfinder** panel, under Shape Modes, **Opt–Click** (MAC) or **Alt–click** (WINDOWS) the **Unite** ( ) button to add the two shapes together. It may not look like anything has happened, but give us a second to prove it.

> ### THE PATHFINDER PANEL
>
> If you just click on any of the Shape Mode operations in Illustrator's Pathfinder panel, the paths are automatically expanded to one shape. To make a compound path, you must **Opt–click** (MAC) or **Alt–click** (WINDOWS) the button in the Pathfinder panel.

13. With the hair still selected, give it:
    – A **3 pt stroke** with a color of **15c, 35m, 100y.**
    – A fill color of **35c, 85m, 85y, 75k.**
    Note: If you don't see CMYK values, go to the **panel menu** ( ) and select **CMYK.**

14. **Deselect** it so you can see how Illustrator now sees the hair as one shape!

15. You can still move the bun separately. Choose the **Group Selection** ( ) tool and make sure only the bun circle is selected. Then move it around and see how the whole thing still looks as though it's one shape.

16. OK, this looks good so far, but our lady is deaf, so let's give her an ear. Using the **Selection** ( ) tool, drag the piece labeled **Ear** into a position appropriate for an ear. Refer to the example if you have to.

17. **Shift–click** on the **face** and in the **Pathfinder** panel, under Shape Modes, click **Unite** ( ).

18. Drag the **Eyebrows** and **Lips** onto the face and position them properly.

19. Drag the **Fan** over so it is partially obscuring her lips.

20. **Deselect** the fan.

21. With the **Group Selection** ( ) tool, click on the **orange part** of the **fan.**

**22.** In the **Appearance** panel **(Window > Appearance)** make the Opacity **70%**.

**23.** Select the entire Geisha and do an **Object > Group.**

**24.** This part of the drawing is complete, so do a **File > Save As** and name it **yourname-geisha.ai**
NOTE: If you get an alert about spot colors and transparency, just click **Continue.**

## MOVING THE ILLUSTRATION ONTO A COVER

**1.** Select the **Geisha** and **Copy** her (**Cmd–C** (MAC) or **Ctrl–C** (WINDOWS)).

**2.** Open the file **MenuCover.ai**

**3.** In the **Layers panel menu** (  ) make sure **Paste Remembers Layers** is **NOT** checked. If it is checked, choose it to turn it off.

**4.** **Paste** the illustration (**Cmd–V** (MAC) or **Ctrl–V** (WINDOWS)).

**5.** Position it into the red area.

**6.** Scale the Geisha **90%** (double-click the **Scale** (  ) tool and enter the amount next to **Uniform**).

**7.** You're done! Save the file as **yourname-MenuCover.ai**
In the dialog that appears, leave the default options checked and click **OK.**

In the future, keep in mind that sometimes you can build an illustration more effectively than drawing it from scratch!

# FINAL PROJECT

FINAL PROJECT

**EXERCISE PREVIEW**

**EXERCISE OVERVIEW**

In this exercise you'll create a hotel brochure. We'll show you how to place multiple graphics, link text from one page to another, set text wrap, as well as how to handle bleed and strokes.

## CREATING THE DOCUMENT

1. Go to **File > New > Document** and set the following:

   – UNcheck **Facing Pages** and **Primary Text Frame.**
   – **4 in** wide by **9 in** tall.
   – Make all the Margins **0.5 in.**
   – Bleed **0.125 in** all around (if you don't see **Bleed,** click **More Options**).

   Click **OK.**

2. In the **InDesign** menu (MAC) or **Edit** menu (WINDOWS), choose **Preferences** and then **Units & Increments.**

3. Change both **Horizontal** and **Vertical** to **Picas.** Click **OK.**

4. Go to **File > Save As** and name it **yourname-sporktown-grand.indd.**

## LAYING OUT THE BACKGROUNDS

1. Go into **File > Place.**

---

**1D**
EXERCISE

2. From **InDesign Class** folder, then **Sporktown Brochure** folder, select **background-pattern.ai** and click **Open.**

3. The cursor should now be a loaded image icon with a preview of the background.

4. Position the top left of this cursor at the **red bleed guide** (which is ⅛ **in** off the top left of the page) and click **once** to place the background.

5. Choose the **Rectangle Frame** ( ) tool.

6. Click and drag a rectangle from the top left bleed to the bottom right bleed.

7. In the **Control** panel, click the **bottom center** reference point ( ).

8. Enter an **H** (Height) of **46p4** and hit **Return** (MAC) or **Enter** (WINDOWS) to make the change.

9. Make sure the rectangle is still selected.

10. Open the **Swatches** panel **(Window > Color > Swatches).**

11. As shown below, at the top left of the **Swatches** panel make sure the **fill** swatch is in front (active). If it's not, click it to make it active.

CLICK HERE ⟶

12. Now we can create the gradient swatch. From the **Swatches panel menu** ( ) at the top right, choose **New Gradient Swatch.**

13. Enter the following:
    Swatch Name: **text background**
    Type: **Linear**

14. In the **Gradient Ramp** section, click on the left slider ( ) to select it.

15. Make sure the **Stop Color** is set to CMYK and set the color:
    **48% Cyan, 47% Magenta, 60% Yellow, 16% Black.**

16. In the **Gradient Ramp** section, click on the right slider ( ) to select it.

17. Make sure the **Stop Color** is set to CMYK and set the color:
    **63% Cyan, 62% Magenta, 67% Yellow, 57% Black.**

    Click **OK.**

18. Make sure the rectangle is still selected.

19. Choose the **Gradient Swatch** ( ) tool.

20. **Hold Shift** and **click and drag** from the top of the rectangle to the bottom.

21. Go to **Object > Effects > Drop Shadow.**

**22.** Check on **Preview** and set the following:

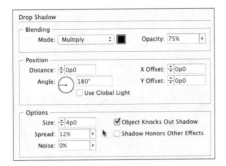

Click **OK.**

**23.** Open the **Pages** panel **(Window > Pages).**

**24.** Select page 1.

**25.** Hold **Option** (MAC) or **Alt** (WINDOWS) and click and drag page 1 down, then let go to make a copy of the page as shown on the right.

**26.** Choose the **Selection** ( ▮ ) tool.

**27.** On page 2, move the gradient box up to the top of the bleed guide.

**28.** In the **Control** panel, make sure the **top left** reference point ( ▦ ) is chosen.

**29.** In the **Control** panel change the **H** (Height) to **44p3** to make it a little shorter.

---

**( MAKING THE FRONT PAGE )**

**1.** Scroll up to **page 1.**

**2.** Click in the empty space off the page to make sure nothing is selected.

**3.** Go to **File > Place.**

**4.** From the **Sporktown Brochure** folder, choose **Sporktown-grand-logo.ai** and click **Open.**

**5.** The cursor should now have the image loaded.
At the top center of the page, click once to place the logo.

**6.** Move the logo so the bottom of the spork sits near the top of the gradient rectangle and is centered between the margins, as shown on the right.

**7.** With the logo still selected, **Shift–Click** the pattern.

**8.** Open the **Align** panel **(Window > Object & Layout > Align).**

**9.** Click the **Align Horizontal Centers** ( ▦ ) button.

**10.** Click off to the side to make sure nothing is selected again and go to **File > Place.**

**1D**

11. From the **Sporktown Brochure** folder, choose **hotel-exterior.tif.**

12. Click once off the left side of the page, but make sure you don't accidentally click into the gradient rectangle! The cursor should be ( 🖊 ) not ( 🖊 ).

13. Enter **X: -0p9** and **Y: 14p3**

### MAKING THE BACK PAGE

1. Scroll to **page 2.**

2. Click off the left side to make sure nothing is selected.

3. Go to **File > Place.**

4. Hold **Cmd** (MAC) or **Ctrl** (WINDOWS), and select the following 3 files:
   - **coastline.psd**
   - **martinis.ai**
   - **no-smoking.ai**

   Click **Open.**

5. The 3 images should now be loaded in the cursor with a number 3 next to the cursor ( 🖊 (3) ) and a preview of the image. The number shows how many images are loaded to place. The currently loaded image should be the **coastline** photo (if not, press any arrow key until it is).

   Click **once off the left side** of the page to place the photo.

6. The cursor should now display (2) and show a preview of the martinis image.

   Click **once off the RIGHT side** of the page to store the martinis for later use.

7. Click once more **at the bottom** of the page in the middle of the pattern section to place the **no-smoking sign.**

8. Move the **coastline** photo to the top of the page, fitting into the margin guides.

### BRING IN THE TEXT

To save time we've already typed and styled all the text for you in a separate InDesign file.

1. Go to **File > Open** and choose the InDesign file **Sporktown-text.indd.**

2. Choose the **Type** ( T ) tool.

3. Click inside the **top** text frame and press **Cmd–A** (MAC) or **Ctrl–A** (WINDOWS) to select all the text.

4. **Copy it (Cmd–C** (MAC) or **Ctrl–C** (WINDOWS)).

5. Switch back to the **yourname-sporktown-grand** file.

6. Go to **page 1.**

7. Inside the margin guides below the photo, click and drag a box following the margin guides to the bottom of the page. Leave some space between the photo and text.

8. **Paste** the text **(Cmd–V** MAC **or Ctrl–V** WINDOWS **).**

9. Notice the red text overflow symbol ( ⊞ ) on the bottom right of the text frame. That means there's too much text to fit inside this box. We want the extra text to flow from this box to the back page.

10. Go down to **page 2.**

11. Inside the margin guides below the photo, click and drag another box following the guides to the end of the gradient box.

12. Go back up to **page 1.**

13. Choose the **Selection** ( ⬏ ) tool.

14. **Click** directly on the text overflow symbol ( ⊞ ). The cursor will load up a preview of that box's text.

15. Scroll down to **page 2.**

16. Position the cursor over the text box you just created, and when it changes into a chain ( 🔗 ), click to link the boxes. The text should flow freely from page 1 to 2.

17. Switch back to the **sporktown-text** file. If you closed it earlier, open it again.

18. Choose the **Type** ( T ) tool.

19. Select the text (not the box) at the bottom of the page.

20. **Copy** it **(Cmd–C** MAC **or Ctrl–C** WINDOWS **).**

21. Switch back to the **yourname-sporktown-grand** file.

22. Make sure that you are on **page 2.**

23. At the bottom of the page, click and drag a new text box filling the margins over the pattern (below the gradient).

24. **Paste** the text **(Cmd–V** MAC **or Ctrl–V** WINDOWS **)** into the box.

**( TEXT WRAP )**

The text is covering over the no-smoking graphic at the bottom. Fortunately we can easily fix that with text wrap.

1. Choose the **Selection** ( ⬏ ) tool.

2. Try to select the no-smoking image.
   If the text is on top of the image, you'll find that you can't click to select the image beneath.

3. Hold **Cmd** (MAC) **or Ctrl** (WINDOWS) and click on the no-smoking image.

   NOTE: Holding **Cmd** (MAC) **or Ctrl** (WINDOWS) lets you click through boxes to whatever is underneath. It might take a few clicks to select the no-smoking sign.

4. Go to **Object > Arrange > Bring to Front** to move it in front.

5. Open the **Text Wrap** panel **(Window > Text Wrap).**

6. At the top of the panel, click the **Jump Object** (  ) button.
   This will make the text jump to the line below the image.

7. Make the text frame taller, it's OK that it goes below the bottom margin guide.

8. Position the no-smoking sign so that the text jumps after **"smoke-free resort."**

9. The no-smoking sign is too large. Do the following:
   - Hold **Cmd–Shift** (MAC) **or Ctrl–Shift** (WINDOWS)
   - Position the cursor over the bottom right resize handle.
   - Click and hold for about 2 seconds before you move the mouse to resize the graphic.
   - Resize it down to roughly ¾ the size of a pattern element.

   TIP: Holding the mouse down for a bit before you move it lets you see a live preview of the image, otherwise you just see the bounding box. Holding **Cmd** (MAC) **or Ctrl** (WINDOWS) lets you resize the box and the image inside at the same time.

10. With the no-smoking sign selected, **Shift-click** the surrounding text to select it too.

11. Visually center it between the top and the bottom of the pattern area.

12. Go to **Window > Object & Layout > Align.**

13. As shown on the right, from the **Align To** menu choose **Align to Page.**

14. Click the **Align Horizontal Centers** (  ) button to make sure everything is centered in the middle of the page.

15. Select the martinis.

16. Go to **Object > Arrange > Bring to Front** so we can easily select them in the future (they were created earlier and therefore would be behind the text).

17. Move them over the lower right corner of the body text.

**18.** Open the **Text Wrap** panel **(Window > Text Wrap)** and set the options as shown.

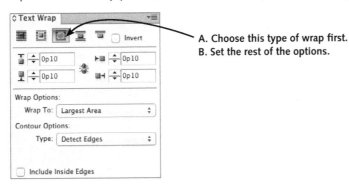

A. **Choose this type of wrap first.**
B. **Set the rest of the options.**

NOTE: Choosing Detect edges wraps the text around the edges of the artwork, not the box.

**19.** Move the martinis around until you get it looking nice. You should be able to get everything fitting together nicely as shown.

**20.** Press **W** to switch into Preview mode and enjoy your work.

## BONUS GOODIES (IF YOU HAVE EXTRA TIME)

**1.** Press **W** to switch back to **Normal** mode.

**2.** Go to **page 1.**

**3.** Choose the **Type** (  ) tool.

**4.** Below the **Sporktown Grand** logo, click and drag a box from margin to margin.

**5.** Go to **Type > Glyphs.**
NOTE: The Glyphs panel shows all the available characters for any given font.

**6.** At the bottom left of the **Glyphs** panel, from the font menu choose **Wingdings.**

**7.** Scroll down until you locate the **star** ( ★ ) and **double-click** it. You should see the star appear in the text box. (If you can't find the star, make sure the Show menu at the top says **Entire Font.)**

**8.** In the **Glyphs** panel, **double-click** the star **3** more times to have **4** stars total.

**9.** Select the stars.

**10.** In the **Control** panel, center ( ☰ ) the stars and make them size **14 pt.**

**11.** Open the **Swatches** panel **(Window > Color > Swatches)**.

**12.** Give them the **light brown** color swatch.

**13.** Select the **hotel exterior** photo.

**14.** In the **Control** panel, make the Stroke weight **2 pt.**

15. In the **Swatches** panel, make sure the **stroke** swatch is in front ( ). If it's not, click it to make it active.

16. We want the same color stroke as the logo, but we don't have that color yet. From the **Swatches panel menu** ( ) at the top right, choose **New Color Swatch.**

17. Leave **Name with Color Value** checked and set the following:

    Color Type: **Process**
    Color Mode: **CMYK**
    Make the color: **47% Cyan, 67% Magenta, 78% Yellow, 55% Black**

    Click **OK.**

18. Open the **Stroke** panel.

19. The stroke doesn't quite go off the edge of our bleed, so for safety's sake click the **Align Stroke to Outside** button.

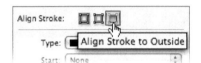

20. Go to **page 2.**

21. Select the **coastline** photo.

22. Open the **Swatches** panel.

23. Make sure the **stroke** icon is active and give it a **[Paper]** color stroke.

24. Open the **Stroke** panel.

25. Give it a **5 pt** stroke.

26. As shown below, click the **Align Stroke to Inside** button.

27. Go into **View > Display Performance > High Quality Display.**

28. Take a look at the pattern at the bottom. Notice that it doesn't quite line up perfectly in the corners?

29. Select the pattern.

30. Move it down until the pattern's squares fit perfectly into the corners, like they do on the top of page 1.

31. Press **W** to switch into Preview mode and enjoy your work.

32. That's it! You've mastered this piece.

# REFERENCE MATERIAL

nobledesktop.com

## ADJUST FONT SIZE
Increase by Increment (set in Preferences)..................................... Ctrl-Shift->
Decrease by Increment ............................................................... Ctrl-Shift-<
(add Alt to the above keystrokes to make them Increment x 5)

## ADJUST LEADING
Increase by Increment (set in Preferences)..................................... Alt-down arrow
Decrease by Increment .................................................................. Alt-up arrow
(add Control to the above keystrokes to make them Increment x 5)
Revert to Auto Leading.................................................................. Ctrl-Alt-Shift-A

## ADJUST KERNING/TRACKING & WORD SPACING
Increase by Increment (set in Preferences)..................................... Alt-right arrow
Decrease by Increment ..................................................................Alt-left arrow
(add Control to the above keystrokes to make them Increment x 5)
Increase between words.................................................................. Ctrl-Alt-Shift-\
Decrease between words..................................................Ctrl-Alt-Shift-Backspace
Clear all manual kerning, tracking, and word spacing ............................ Ctrl-Alt-Q

## ADJUST BASELINE SHIFT
Move Up by Increment (set in Preferences)............................. Alt-Shift-up arrow
Move Down by Increment................................................. Alt-Shift-down arrow
(add Control to the above keystrokes to make them Increment x 5)

## SCALING PICTURES
**MAKE SURE THE PICTURE CONTENT IS SELECTED (NOT THE FRAME THAT IT'S INSIDE)**
Scale 5% Bigger ........................................................................... Ctrl-Alt->
Scale 5% Smaller .......................................................................... Ctrl-Alt-<
Scale 1% Bigger ........................................................................... Ctrl->
Scale 1% Smaller .......................................................................... Ctrl-<

## FITTING CONTENT & PICTURES
Fit Content Proportionally .......................................................... Ctrl-Alt-Shift-E
Fill Frame Proportionally.............................................................. Ctrl-Alt-Shift-C
Center Content ........................................................................... Ctrl-Shift-E
Fit Frame to Content ................................................................... Ctrl-Alt-C

## NUDGING OBJECTS
Move by Increment (set in Preferences) .........................................any arrow key
Move by Increment x 10.......................................................Shift-any arrow key
Move by Increment x 1/10.................................................Ctrl-Shift-any arrow key

## FLOWING TEXT
🔃 Multi-Page Autoflow (creates additional pages) ..................................Shift-click
🔃 Semi-autoflow (keeps text in cursor so you can continue flowing).........Alt-click
↓ Fixed-Page Autoflow (does not create additional pages) ...............Shift-Alt-click

## STYLING TEXT & WORKING WITH STYLES
Bold: Ctrl-Shift-B • Italic: Ctrl-Shift-I • Normal: Ctrl-Shift-Y • All Caps: Ctrl-Shift-K
Edit Style Sheet without Applying it .......................Ctrl-Alt-Shift-Double click style
Redefine a Paragraph Style ................................................ Ctrl-Alt–Shift-R
Redefine a Character Style ................................................. Ctrl-Alt–Shift-C

## WORKING WITH PARAGRAPH STYLES
To remove local formatting (non Style changes) ................... Alt-click Style Name
To remove local formatting and Character Styles .......... Alt-Shift-click Style Name

## WORKING WITH MASTER PAGES
Override a single master page item on a document page .............Ctrl-Shift-click it
Override several master page items ............. Ctrl-Shift-drag a marquee over them
Override all master page items on pages selected in Pages panel .....Ctrl-Alt-Shift-L

## INSERT SPECIAL CHARACTERS
Indent to Here.............................................................................. Ctrl-\
Right Indent Tab ......................................................................... Shift-Tab
Discretionary Hyphen....................................................Ctrl-Shift-hyphen (-)
Nonbreaking Hyphen ..................................................... Ctrl-Alt-hyphen (-)
Type in Single Straight Quote (Foot Mark) ..........................................Alt-'
Type in Double Straight Quote (Inch Mark) ....................................Alt-Shift-'
Current Page Number (Auto Page Numbering).............................Ctrl-Alt-Shift-N

## INSERT WHITE SPACE
Em space...................................................................................... Ctrl-Shift-M
En space....................................................................................... Ctrl-Shift-N
Nonbreaking space ...................................................................... Ctrl-Alt-X
Thin space ................................................................................... Ctrl-Alt-Shift-M

## INSERT BREAK CHARACTERS
Column Break............................................................. Enter (on keypad)
Frame Break ....................................................Shift-Enter (on keypad)

Page Break............................................................. Ctrl-Enter (on keypad)
Forced Line Break (or "soft return") .............................................Shift-Enter

## MOVING TEXT CURSOR
Move cursor to beginning or end of line ..........................................Home or End
Move cursor one word to the left/right................................Ctrl-Left/right arrow
Move cursor to Previous paragraph ............................................ Ctrl-Up Arrow
Move cursor to Next paragraph ................................................ Ctrl-Down Arrow

## SELECTING & WORKING WITH TEXT
Leave Text Frame and switch to Selection tool............................................. Esc
Select from cursor to beginning or end of line .................Shift-Home or Shift-End
Select from cursor to end of story ......................................... Ctrl-Shift-End
Select from cursor to beginning of story .............................. Ctrl-Shift-Home
Select whole word ..................................................................Double-click
Select line ...............................................Ctrl-Shift-\ (or Triple-click)
Select one word to the left/right ....................Ctrl-Shift-Left/Right arrow

## NAVIGATING & SCROLLING THROUGH DOCUMENTS
Scroll using Hand tool ...............................................Alt-Spacebar-Drag
Go to the First Page .......................................... Ctrl-Shift-Page Up
Go to the Last Page ..........................................Ctrl-Shift-Page Down
Go to Page (then type in page number) .......................................Ctrl-J
Switch between open Documents..................................Ctrl-tilde(~)

## ZOOMING
Get the Zoom in tool without selecting it............................... Hold Ctrl then Space
Get the Zoom out tool without selecting it.................Hold Ctrl then Space and Alt
Zoom In or Out ..........................................Ctrl-plus(+) or Ctrl-minus(–)
Fit Page in Window .......................................................Ctrl-0 (zero)
Fit Spread in Window ..............................................Ctrl-Alt-0 (zero)
Toggle between current and previous zoom levels ................................ Ctrl-Alt-2

## FIND/CHANGE
Insert selected text into Find What box ...........................................Ctrl-F1
Insert selected text into Find What box and then Find Next instance .......Shift-F1
Find the next occurrence of Find What text......................... Shift-F2 or Ctrl-Alt-F
Insert selected text into Change To box ...........................................Ctrl-F2
Replace selected text with Change To text.......................................... Ctrl-F3
Replace selected text with Change To text and Find Next.......................Shift-F3

## WORKING WITH PANELS
Highlight the first option in the Control panel .......................................... Ctrl-6
Toggle Control panel between Character & Paragraph options .......... Ctrl-Alt-7
Apply a value but keep it highlighted in panel .....................................Shift-Enter
Show/Hide all Panels including Toolbox .................Tab (while not in a text frame)
Show/Hide all Panels except the Toolbox ........Shift-Tab (while not in a text frame)
Expand/Collapse Panel Stacks........... Ctrl-Alt-Shift-Tab (while not in a text frame)
Create new (style, swatches, etc) & display options dialog ..... Alt-click New button

## WORKING WITH DIALOG BOXES
Rotate down through section of options displayed on the left...............Page Down
Rotate up through section of options displayed on the left......................Page Up
Jump to section of options displayed on the left ..Ctrl-1 for 1st, Ctrl-2 for 2nd, etc.
Choose Yes or No................................................................................... Y or N

## MISCELLANEOUS GOOD STUFF
Select frame hidden behind another........ Hold Ctrl and keep clicking frame stack
Increase/decrease a value in a field.................click in field, press up/down arrow
Highlight the Last Used Field (in a panel) ................................... Ctrl-Alt-tilde(~)
In Tabs panel: Move Left Indent (triangle) without moving First Line Indent ..........
............................................Hold Shift while dragging the (bottom) triangle
Select all Guides ............................................................................Ctrl-Alt-G
Select an Individual Table Cell ..................With Type tool, click in cell and hit Esc
Quick Apply ............................... Press Ctrl-Enter. Then start typing a style name,
menu item, text variable, etc. Then press Enter to apply.
Sort Menus Alphabetically ...........................Hold Ctrl-Alt-Shift and click on Menu
Toggle Typographer's Quotes preference......................................... Ctrl-Alt-Shift-'

## TOOLS

| | |
|---|---|
| V | Move |
| M | Marquee tools |
| L | Lasso tools |
| W | Quick Selection, Magic Wand |
| C | Crop and Slice tools |
| I | Eyedropper, Color Sampler, Ruler, Note, Count |
| J | Spot Healing Brush, Healing Brush, Patch, Red Eye |
| B | Brush, Pencil, Color Replacement, Mixer Brush |
| S | Clone Stamp, Pattern Stamp |
| Y | History Brush, Art History Brush |
| E | Eraser tools |
| G | Gradient, Paint Bucket |
| O | Dodge, Burn, Sponge |
| P | Pen tools |
| T | Type tools |
| A | Path Selection, Direct Selection |
| U | Rectangle, Rounded Rectangle, Ellipse, Polygon, Line, Custom Shape |
| K | 3D tools |
| N | 3D Camera tools |
| H | Hand |
| R | Rotate |
| Z | Zoom |
| D | Default colors |
| X | Switch Foreground and Background colors |
| Q | Quick Mask Mode |

## SWITCHING TOOLS

To switch between all tools within groups, add the Shift key to the letters above.
For example, to switch between rectangular and elliptical marquee..........Shift-M

## SELECTING

Draw Marquee from Center ................................................ Alt-Marquee
Add to a Selection ................................................................... Shift
Subtract from a Selection ................................................................... Alt
Intersection with a Selection ......................................................... Shift-Alt
Make Copy of Selection w/Move tool .................................Alt-Drag Selection
Make Copy of Selection when not in Move tool................. Ctrl-Alt-Drag Selection
Move Selection (in 1-pixel Increments) ....................................Arrow Keys
Move Selection (in 10-pixel Increments) ...............................Shift-Arrow Keys
Select all Opaque Pixels on Layer ..... Ctrl-click on Layer Thumbnail (in Layers panel)
Restore Last Selection ........................................................ Ctrl-Shift-D
Feather Selection ...................................................................... Shift-F6
Move Marquee while drawing selection..........Hold Space while drawing marquee

## VIEWING

Fit on Screen ...............................................Double-click on Hand tool or Ctrl-0
100% View Level (Actual Pixels)............. Double-Click on Zoom Tool or Ctrl-Alt-0
Zoom in ............................................................Ctrl-Space-Click or Ctrl-Plus(+)
Zoom out .....................................................Alt-Space-Click or Ctrl-Minus(–)
Hide all tools and panels...............................................................Tab
Hide all panels except Toolbox and Options bar ....................................Shift-Tab
Rotate through full screen modes ..................................................F
Scroll image left or right in window ..............................Ctrl-Shift-Page Up/Down
Jump/Zoom to part of Image ..........................Ctrl-drag in Navigator panel
Toggles layer mask on/off as rubylith.................................................\

## LAYER SHORTCUTS

Create new layer ..................................................................Ctrl-Shift-N
Select non-contiguous layers ....................................................Ctrl-Click layers
Select contiguous layers ..................Click one layer, then Shift-Click another layer
Delete Layer ...........................................Delete key (while in the Move tool)
View contents of layer mask ...........................................Alt-Click layer mask icon
Temporarily turn off layer mask....................................Shift-Click layer mask icon
Clone layer as you move it..................................................... Alt-Drag
Find/Select layer containing object .............Right-Click on the object w/Move tool
Change layer opacity ............................Number pad keys (w/Move tool selected)
Cycle down or up through blend modes........................ Shift-Plus(+) or Minus(–)
Change to a specific blend mode
..................................... (w/Move tool) Shift-Alt-letter (ie: N=Normal, M=Multiply. etc.)
Switch to layer below/above current layer...........................................Alt-[ or Alt-]
Move layer below/above current layer ...........................................Ctrl-[ or Ctrl-]

## TYPE SHORTCUTS

Select all text on layer..................... Double-Click on T thumbnail in Layers panel
Increase/Decrease size of selected text by 2 pts.............................Ctrl-Shift->/<
Increase/Decrease size of selected text by 10 pts.......................Ctrl-Shift-Alt->/<
Increase/Decrease kerning/tracking.....................................Alt-Right/Left Arrow
Align text left/center/right.............................................Ctrl-Shift-L/C/R

## PAINTING

Fill selection with background color .........................................Ctrl-Backspace
Fill selection with foreground color.........................................Alt-Backspace
Fill selection with foreground color using Lock Transparent Pixels
...................................................................Shift-Alt-Backspace
Fill selection with source state in History panel .......................Ctrl-Alt-Backspace
Display Fill dialog box...........................................................Shift-Backspace
Sample as background color ....................................Alt-Click w/Eyedropper tool
To get Move tool ..................................While in any painting/editing tool-hold Ctrl
To get Eyedropper with Paint tools ...............................................................Alt
Change paint opacity (with Airbrush OFF)........................... Number keys
Change paint opacity (with Airbrush ON) ................................Shift-Number keys
Change Airbrush flow (with Airbrush ON) ...................................... Number keys
Change Airbrush flow (with Airbrush OFF) ...........................Shift-Number keys
Cross-Hair Cursor............................. Any painting/editing tool-turn Caps Lock on
Decrease/Increase Brush Size................................................... [ or ]
Decrease/Increase Hardness of Brush............................... Shift-[ or Shift-]
Switch between preset Brushes ....................................................< or >
Open Brushes pop-up panel ...................................Right-Click in Image window
Erase to History panel's source state..............................................Alt-Eraser
Cycle down or up through blend modes........................ Shift-Plus(+) or Minus(–)
Change to a specific blend mode.... Shift-Alt-letter (ie: N=Normal, M=Multiply, etc.)
Create fixed color target from within a dialog box ....... Shift-Click in image window
Delete fixed color target......................Alt-Click on target with Color Sampler tool
Create new spot-color channel from current selection
...................................Ctrl-Click on New Channel button in Channels panel

## PEN TOOL SHORTCUTS

To get Direct Selection tool while using Pen ...........................................Ctrl
Switch between Add-Anchor and Delete-Anchor Point tools...........................Alt
Switch from Path Selection tool to Convert Point tool when
pointer is over anchor point ...................................................... Ctrl-Alt
To Select a whole path w/Direct Selection tool .........................................Alt-click
Convert path to a selection ....................Ctrl-click on path name (in Paths panel)

## PANEL SHORTCUTS

Show/Hide Brushes panel ...................................................................F5
Show/Hide Color panel.......................................................................F6
Show/Hide Layers panel .....................................................................F7
Show/Hide Info panel .........................................................................F8
Show/Hide Actions panel.............................................................Alt-F9
Open Adobe Bridge...................................................................Ctrl-Alt-O

## OTHER SHORTCUTS

Switch between open documents ...............................................Ctrl-Tab
Undo or Redo operations beyond last one .................Ctrl-Alt-Z/Ctrl-Shift-Z
Apply Last Filter ...............................................................................Ctrl-F
Opens Last Filter Dialog Box.............................................................Ctrl-Alt-F
Hand Tool ......................................................................................Spacebar
Reset Dialog Box........................Hold Alt, Cancel turns into Reset Button, Click it
Increase/Decrease value (in any option field) by 1 unit................Up/Down Arrow
Increase/Decrease value (in any option field) by 10 units .....Shift-Up/Down Arrow
Replay last Transformation .............................................. Ctrl-Shift-T
Measure Angle between Lines (Protractor Function)
...................................... After ruler is drawn, Alt-Drag end of line with Ruler Tool
Move Crop Marquee while creating.............................Hold Space while drawing
Snap Guide to Ruler ticks.............................................Hold Shift while dragging
Highlight Fields in Options bar (n/a for all tools) .........................................Enter
Don't Snap object edge while moving ........................Hold Control while dragging

NOBLE DESKTOP LLC, 594 BROADWAY, SUITE 1202, NEW YORK, NY 10012   PHONE: 212-226-4149

## TOOLS

| | |
|---|---|
| V..........Selection | E...........Free Transform |
| A .........Direct Selection | Shift-S...Symbol Sprayer |
| Y..........Magic Wand | J............Column Graph |
| Q..........Lasso | U..........Mesh |
| P...........Pen | G..........Gradient |
| + .........Add Anchor point | I............Eyedropper |
| - ..........Delete Anchor point | W..........Blend |
| Shift-C ..Convert Anchor point | K ..........Live Paint Bucket |
| T..........Type | Shift-L...Live Paint Selection |
| \...........Line Segment | Shift-O ..Artboard |
| M..........Rectangle | Shift-K ..Slice |
| L...........Ellipse | H...........Hand |
| B .........Paintbrush | Z..........Zoom |
| N .........Pencil | X...........Toggle between Fill & Stroke |
| Shift-B ..Blob Brush | Shift-X...Swap Fill & Stroke |
| Shift-E...Eraser | D .........Default Fill & Stroke |
| C ..........Scissors |  (white fill/black stroke) |
| R .........Rotate | < ..........Fill or Stroke w/Color |
| O ..........Reflect | > ..........Fill or Stroke w/Gradient |
| S..........Scale | /...........Fill or Stroke w/None |
| Shift-R ..Warp | F..........Cycle through Screen Modes |

Double-click tools to bring up options.
Press CAPS LOCK to change tool pointer to crosshair.
Hold down Shift to constrain movement to 45°, 90°, 135°, or 180°.

## SELECTING AND MOVING

To access Selection or Direction Selection tool (whichever was used last)
    at any time .........................................................Control
To switch between Selection and Direct Selection tools .....................Ctrl-Alt-Tab
To cycle through tools behind column tool .......................................Alt-click tool
To make copy while dragging...........................................................Alt
To add to a selection ...................................................................... Shift
Move Selection................................................................ Any arrow key
Move Selection 10 pts.......................................Shift-any arrow key
Lock selected artwork......................................................... Ctrl-2
Lock all deselected artwork .........................................Ctrl-Alt-Shift-2
Unlock all artwork .........................................................Ctrl-Alt-2
Hide selected artwork....................................................... Ctrl-3
Hide all deselected artwork ..........................................Ctrl-Alt-Shift-3
Show all artwork............................................................Ctrl-Alt-3

## PATH EDITING

Join and Average at same time ............................Ctrl-Alt-Shift-J
Convert Anchor Point tool from Pen tool ...................................... Alt
Switch between Add Anchor Point and Delete Anchor Point tools....................Alt
Add Anchor Point tool from Scissors tool ......................................... Alt
Move anchor point while drawing with Pen tool.................................... Spacebar
Create closed path with Pencil or Paintbrush tool..........................
    ................................... when finished drawing, hold Alt and release mouse
Connect to an open (& selected) path with Pencil ....................Ctrl-drag

## PAINTING AND TRANSFORMING

Eyedropper tool from Live Paint Bucket tool ..................................... Alt
Samples intermediate color from gradient, picture, etc. with eyedropper ....... Shift
Sets center point and shows dialog......................... Alt-click with Tool
Duplicates and transforms selection ......................................Alt-drag
Transform pattern without transforming object ................................~(tilde)-drag
Scale proportionally with Selection tool ......................... Shift-drag bounding box
Scale from center with Selection tool .............................. Alt-drag bounding box
Move mesh point along path with Mesh tool ................................. Shift-drag
Add mesh point with Mesh tool without changing color ....................... Shift-click
Remove mesh point with Mesh tool .....................................Alt-click

## SHAPES (WHILE DRAWING)

Draw from center ........................................................................ Alt
Draw from center with dialog ...................................................Alt-click
Constrain proportion........................................................... Shift
Constrain orientation of polygons, stars, spirals ...................................... Shift
Move object while drawing ........................................................... Spacebar
Add/subtract sides, points, spiral segments ...........................Up or Down Arrow
Decrease inner radius .....................................................................Ctrl
Create continuous duplicates along mouse movement ........ hold ~ while dragging

## VIEWING & GUIDES

Get Hand Tool (while NOT editing Type) ................................................. Spacebar
Get Hand tool (while editing Type) .........Hold Control, then Space. (This will show
    the Zoom tool). Let go of Control so you see the Hand tool and IMMEDIATELY
    start dragging the mouse so you don't end up typing spaces. Be sure to let go
    of the Spacebar *while* dragging so you again don't type more spaces.
Zoom In Tool ...................................................................... Ctrl-Spacebar
Zoom Out Tool .......................................................... Ctrl-Alt-Spacebar
Zoom In to exact size .......................................... Ctrl-Spacebar-drag
Hide/Show all tools and panels.................................................................. Tab
Hide/Show all panels except toolbox ................................................ Shift-Tab
Switch between horizontal/vertical guide ...hold Alt while dragging out a new guide
Release Guide (turns it into a regular path).........................Shift-Ctrl-double-click

## TYPE

Decrease/Increase type size ..................................................... Ctrl-Shift-< or >
Decrease/Increase leading ............................................... Alt arrow up or down
Decrease/Increase kerning/tracking.............................. Alt arrow left or right
Kerning/tracking x 5 ...........................................Ctrl-Alt arrow left or right
Decrease/Increase baseline shift ...................... Shift-Alt arrow down or up
Baseline shift x 5.................................Ctrl-Alt-Shift arrow down or up
Align type left, right, center........................................Ctrl-Shift-L, R, C
Justify type............................................................................Ctrl-Shift-J
Justify last line ......................................................................Ctrl-Shift-F
Reset horizontal/vertical scale to 100%....................................Ctrl-Shift-X
Reset kerning or tracking to 0...............................................Ctrl-Alt-Q

## PANEL SHORTCUTS/FUNCTION KEYS

Show/Hide Brushes .......................................................................F5
Show/Hide Color ..........................................................................F6
Show/Hide Layers .........................................................................F7
Show/Hide Info .................................................................... Ctrl-F8
Show/Hide Gradient .............................................................. Ctrl-F9
Show/Hide Stroke................................................................. Ctrl-F10
Show/Hide Attributes............................................................. Ctrl-F11
Revert file ...........................................................................F12
Show/Hide Graphic Styles ..................................................... Shift-F5
Show/Hide Appearance ........................................................Shift-F6
Show/Hide Align......................................................................Shift-F7
Show/Hide Transform .............................................................Shift-F8
Show/Hide Pathfinder .......................................................Shift-Ctrl-F9
Show/Hide Transparency....................................................Shift-Ctrl-F10
Show/Hide Symbols .........................................................Shift-Ctrl-F11

## LAYERS PANEL SHORTCUTS

Toggle layer between Preview/Outline mode..............................Ctrl-click on eye
Show layer while turning-off all others................................Alt-click on eye
Select all items on layer ......................................Alt-click layer name
Copy selected item to different layer ........Alt-drag selection square in Layers panel
To create the new layer at the top of list ............................... Ctrl-click
To create the new layer below selected layer ...................................Ctrl-Alt-click

## COLOR PANEL SHORTCUTS

Saturate/Desaturate current color ..........................Shift-drag color slider
Change Color Mode..........................................Shift-click color bar
Select compliment of current color ........................................Ctrl-click color bar

## SWATCHES PANEL SHORTCUTS

Create a swatch as a global color............................Hold Crtl–Shift while creating
Replace a swatch with another ................................. Alt-drag new swatch over old

## MISC.

(In any panel) Apply a value, but keep value highlighted in panel...... Shift-Return
Create New Symbol............................................................................F8
Swap Colors in a Gradient ................................Alt-Drag a color stop onto another

# InDesign CS6

## Useful Keyboard Shortcuts: Mac

nobledesktop.com

### ADJUST FONT SIZE

Increase by Increment (set in Preferences)................................⌘-Shift->
Decrease by Increment .................................................⌘-Shift-<
(add Option to the above keystrokes to make them Increment x 5)

### ADJUST LEADING

Increase by Increment (set in Preferences)...........................Option-down arrow
Decrease by Increment .................................................Option-up arrow
(add ⌘ to the above keystrokes to make them Increment x 5)
Revert to Auto Leading ..............................................⌘-Option-Shift-A

### ADJUST KERNING/TRACKING & WORD SPACING

Increase by Increment (set in Preferences)...........................Option-right arrow
Decrease by Increment ................................................Option-left arrow
(add ⌘ to the above keystrokes to make them Increment x 5)
Increase between words ............................................⌘-Option-Shift-\
Decrease between words......................................⌘-Option-Shift-Delete
Clear all manual kerning, tracking, and word spacing ......................⌘-Option-Q

### ADJUST BASELINE SHIFT

Move Up by Increment (set in Preferences).....................Option-Shift-up arrow
Move Down by Increment........................................Option-Shift-down arrow
(add ⌘ to the above keystrokes to make them Increment x 5)

### SCALING PICTURES

**MAKE SURE THE PICTURE CONTENT IS SELECTED (NOT THE FRAME THAT IT'S INSIDE)**

Scale 5% Bigger ....................................................⌘-Opt->
Scale 5% Smaller ...................................................⌘-Opt-<
Scale 1% Bigger ......................................................⌘->
Scale 1% Smaller ....................................................⌘-<

### FITTING CONTENT & PICTURES

Fit Content Proportionally .........................................⌘-Opt-Shift-E
Fill Frame Proportionally............................................⌘-Opt-Shift-C
Center Content .......................................................⌘-Shift-E
Fit Frame to Content ................................................⌘-Opt-C

### NUDGING OBJECTS

Move by Increment (set in Preferences) ...........................any arrow key
Move by Increment x 10................................................Shift-any arrow key
Move by Increment x 1/10................................................⌘-Shift-any arrow key

### FLOWING TEXT

⌐ᴫ Multi-Page Autoflow (creates additional pages) ......................Shift-click
⌐ᴫ Semi-autoflow (keeps text in cursor so you can continue flowing)...Option-click
↓ Fixed-Page Autoflow (does not create additional pages) .........Shift-Option-click

### STYLING TEXT & WORKING WITH STYLES

Bold: ⌘-Shift-B • Italic: ⌘-Shift-I • Normal: ⌘-Shift-Y • All Caps: ⌘-Shift-K
Edit Style Sheet without Applying it ..................⌘-Option-Shift-Double click style
Redefine a Paragraph Style ........................................⌘-Opt–Shift-R
Redefine a Character Style ........................................⌘-Opt–Shift-C

### WORKING WITH PARAGRAPH STYLES

To remove local formatting (non Style changes) ..................Opt-click Style Name
To remove local formatting and Character Styles ..........Opt-Shift-click Style Name

### WORKING WITH MASTER PAGES

Override a single master page item on a document page .............⌘-Shift-click it
Override several master page items ...............⌘-Shift-drag a marquee over them
Override all master page items on pages selected in Pages panel .....⌘-Opt-Shift-L

### INSERT SPECIAL CHARACTERS

Indent to Here.........................................................⌘-\
Right Indent Tab ....................................................Shift-Tab
Discretionary Hyphen...........................................⌘-Shift-hyphen (-)
Nonbreaking Hyphen ...............................................⌘-Opt-hyphen (-)
Type in Single Straight Quote (Foot Mark) ................................Ctrl-'
Type in Double Straight Quote (Inch Mark) ...........................Ctrl-Shift-'
Current Page Number (Auto Page Numbering)...................⌘-Opt-Shift-N

### INSERT WHITE SPACE

Em space.............................................................⌘-Shift-M
En space.............................................................⌘-Shift-N
Nonbreaking space ..................................................⌘-Opt-X
Thin space ..........................................................⌘-Opt-Shift-M

### INSERT BREAK CHARACTERS

Column Break.........................................Enter (on keypad)
Frame Break.....................................Shift-Enter (on keypad)

Page Break..................................................⌘-Enter (on keypad)
Forced Line Break (or "soft return") ...........................Shift-Return

### MOVING TEXT CURSOR

Move cursor to beginning or end of line.............................Home or End
Move cursor one word to the left/right..........................⌘-Left/right arrow
Move cursor to Previous paragraph ................................⌘-Up Arrow
Move cursor to Next paragraph ....................................⌘-Down Arrow

### SELECTING & WORKING WITH TEXT

Leave Text Frame and switch to Selection tool............................Esc
Select from cursor to beginning or end of line .................Shift-Home or Shift-End
Select from cursor to end of story ................................⌘-Shift-End
Select from cursor to beginning of story .........................⌘-Shift-Home
Select whole word ................................................Double-click
Select line ...............................................⌘-Shift-\ (or Triple-click)
Select one word to the left/right ..........................⌘-Shift-Left/Right arrow

### NAVIGATING & SCROLLING THROUGH DOCUMENTS

Scroll using Hand tool ..........................................Option-Spacebar-Drag
Go to the First Page.............................................⌘-Shift-Page Up
Go to the Last Page..............................................⌘-Shift-Page Down
Go to Page (then type in page number) ...............................⌘-J
Switch between open Documents....................................⌘-tilde(~)

### ZOOMING

Get the Zoom in tool without selecting it...............................Hold ⌘ then Space
Get the Zoom out tool without selecting it............Hold ⌘ then Space and Option
Zoom In or Out ....................................⌘-plus(+) or ⌘-minus(–)
Fit Page in Window ................................................⌘-0 (zero)
Fit Spread in Window .............................................⌘-Option-0 (zero)
Access zoom percentage box so you can enter a zoom level
(Application Frame and Bar must be turned off).........................⌘-Opt-5
Toggle between current and previous zoom levels....................⌘-Opt-2

### FIND/CHANGE

Insert selected text into Find What box ...............................⌘-F1
Insert selected text into Find What box and then Find Next instance .......Shift-F1
Find the next occurrence of Find What text.................Shift-F2 or ⌘-Option-F
Insert selected text into Change To box................................⌘-F2
Replace selected text with Change To text..............................⌘-F3
Replace selected text with Change To text and Find Next.................Shift-F3

### WORKING WITH PANELS

Highlight the first option in the Control panel ............................⌘-6
Toggle Control panel between Character & Paragraph options................⌘-Opt-7
Apply a value but keep it highlighted in panel .................... Shift-Return
Show/Hide all Panels including Toolbox .................Tab (while not in a text frame)
Show/Hide all Panels except the Toolbox ........Shift-Tab (while not in a text frame)
Expand/Collapse Panel Stacks ..........⌘-Opt-Tab (while not in a text frame)
Create new (style, swatches, etc) & display options dialog ....Opt-click New button

### WORKING WITH DIALOG BOXES

Rotate down through section of options displayed on the left..............Page Down
Rotate up through section of options displayed on the left.................Page Up
Jump to section of options displayed on the left.....⌘-1 for 1st, ⌘-2 for 2nd, etc.
Choose Yes, No, Don't Save, or Save .........................Y, N, D, or S

### MISCELLANEOUS GOOD STUFF

Select frame hidden behind another..........Hold ⌘ and keep clicking frame stack
Increase/decrease a value in a field.................click in field, press up/down arrow
Highlight the Last Used Field (in a panel) .........................Cmd-Option-tilde(~)
In Tabs panel: Move Left Indent (triangle) without moving First Line Indent..........
..................................Hold Shift while dragging the (bottom) triangle
Select all Guides ................................................⌘-Opt-G
Select an Individual Table Cell ..................With Type tool, click in cell and hit Esc
Quick Apply .............................. Press ⌘-Return. Then start typing a style name,
.................menu item, text variable, etc. Then press Return to apply.
Sort Menus Alphabetically .......................... Hold ⌘-Opt-Shift and click on Menu
Toggle Typographer's Quotes preference.............................⌘-Opt-Shift-'

noble desktop
Exceptional computer graphics training

NOBLE DESKTOP LLC, 594 BROADWAY, SUITE 1202, NEW YORK, NY 10012
PHONE: 212-226-4149 COPYRIGHT © 2013 NOBLE DESKTOP

nobledesktop.com

## TOOLS

| | |
|---|---|
| V | Move |
| M | Marquee tools |
| L | Lasso tools |
| W | Quick Selection, Magic Wand |
| C | Crop and Slice tools |
| I | Eyedropper, Color Sampler, Ruler, Note, Count |
| J | Spot Healing Brush, Healing Brush, Patch, Red Eye |
| B | Brush, Pencil, Color Replacement, Mixer Brush |
| S | Clone Stamp, Pattern Stamp |
| Y | History Brush, Art History Brush |
| E | Eraser tools |
| G | Gradient, Paint Bucket |
| O | Dodge, Burn, Sponge |
| P | Pen tools |
| T | Type tools |
| A | Path Selection, Direct Selection |
| U | Rectangle, Rounded Rectangle, Ellipse, Polygon, Line, Custom Shape |
| K | 3D tools |
| N | 3D Camera tools |
| H | Hand |
| R | Rotate |
| Z | Zoom |
| D | Default colors |
| X | Switch Foreground and Background colors |
| Q | Quick Mask Mode |

## SWITCHING TOOLS

To switch between all tools within groups, add the Shift key to the letters above.
For example, to switch between rectangular and elliptical marquee..........Shift-M

## SELECTING

Draw Marquee from Center ...........................................................Option-Marquee
Add to a Selection ..................................................................................... Shift
Subtract from a Selection ........................................................................Option
Intersection with a Selection ..........................................................Shift-Option
Make Copy of Selection w/Move tool ......................Option-Drag Selection
Make Copy of Selection when not in Move tool............ ⌘-Option-Drag Selection
Move Selection (in 1-pixel Increments) ............................................ Arrow Keys
Move Selection (in 10-pixel Increments) ................................Shift-Arrow Keys
Select all Opaque Pixels on Layer...... ⌘-Click on Layer Thumbnail (in Layers panel)
Restore Last Selection ...................................................................... ⌘-Shift-D
Feather Selection..........................................................................Shift-F6
Move Marquee while drawing selection..........Hold Space while drawing marquee

## VIEWING

Fit on Screen ...................................................Double-click on Hand tool or ⌘-0
100% View Level (Actual Pixels).......... Double-Click on Zoom Tool or ⌘-Option-0
Zoom in ............................................. ⌘-Space-Click or ⌘-Plus(+)
Zoom out ................................................ Option-Space-Click or ⌘-Minus(–)
Hide all tools and panels ...................................................................... Tab
Hide all panels except Toolbox and Options bar ................................... Shift-Tab
Rotate through full screen modes ............................................................... F
Scroll image left or right in window ......................... ⌘-Shift-Page Up/Down
Jump/Zoom to part of Image ....................................⌘-drag in Navigator panel
Toggles layer mask on/off as rubylith...................................................\

## LAYER SHORTCUTS

Create new layer ........................................................................ ⌘-Shift-N
Select non-contiguous layers ....................................................... ⌘-Click layers
Select contiguous layers .................Click one layer, then Shift-Click another layer
Delete Layer .............................................................................. Delete key
View contents of layer mask .....................................Option-Click layer mask icon
Temporarily turn off layer mask....................................Shift-Click layer mask icon
Clone layer as you move it............................................................ Option-Drag
Find/Select layer containing object ...............Control-Click on object w/Move tool
Change layer opacity .....................................Number keys (w/Move tool selected)
Cycle down or up through blend modes........................ Shift-Plus(+) or Minus(–)
Change to a specific blend mode
.............. (w/Move tool) Shift-Option-letter (ie: N=Normal, M=Multiply. etc.)
Switch to layer below/above current layer............................. Option-[ or Option-]
Move layer below/above current layer ..................................... ⌘-[ or ⌘-]

## TYPE SHORTCUTS

Select all text on layer...................... Double-Click on T thumbnail in Layers panel
Increase/Decrease size of selected text by 2pts.................................⌘-Shift->/<
Increase/Decrease size of selected text by 10 pts..................⌘-Option-Shift->/<
Increase/Decrease kerning/tracking............................... Option-Right/Left Arrow
Align text left/center/right...............................................................⌘-Shift-L/C/R

## PAINTING

Fill selection with background color............................................................⌘-Delete
Fill selection with foreground color...........................................................Option-Delete
Fill selection with foreground color using Lock Transparent Pixels
.........................................................................................Option-Shift-Delete
Fill selection with source state in History panel .........................⌘-Option-Delete
Display Fill dialog box........................................................................ Shift-Delete
Sample as background color .............................Option-Click w/Eyedropper tool
To get Move tool ......................... While in any painting/editing tool-hold ⌘
To get Eyedropper with Paint tools ....................................................Option
Change paint opacity (with Airbrush OFF)............................ Number keys
Change paint opacity (with Airbrush ON) ................................Shift-Number keys
Change Airbrush flow (with Airbrush ON) ............................ Number keys
Change Airbrush flow (with Airbrush OFF) .........................Shift-Number keys
Cross-Hair Cursor............................. Any painting/editing tool-turn Caps Lock on
Decrease/Increase Brush Size.......................................................... [ or ]
Decrease/Increase Hardness of Brush ............................... Shift-[ or Shift-]
Switch between preset Brushes........................................................< or >
Open Brushes pop-up panel ........................................Ctrl-Click in Image window
Erase to History panel's source state..........................................Option-Eraser
Cycle down or up through blend modes........................Shift-Plus(+) or Minus(–)
Change to a specific blend mode...Shift-Opt-letter (ie: N=Normal, M=Multiply, etc.)
Create fixed color target from within a dialog box ....... Shift-Click in image window
Delete fixed color target.................Option-Click on target with Color Sampler tool
Create new spot-color channel from current selection
.................................... ⌘-Click on New Channel button in Channels panel

## PEN TOOL SHORTCUTS

To get Direct Selection tool while using Pen .......................................... ⌘
Switch between Add-Anchor and Delete-Anchor Point tools ......................Option
Switch from Path Selection tool to Convert Point tool when
        pointer is over anchor point ........................................... ⌘-Option
To Select a whole path w/Direct Selection tool ............................Option-click
Convert path to a selection ......................⌘-click on path name (in Paths panel)

## PANEL SHORTCUTS

Show/Hide Brushes panel ........................................................................F5
Show/Hide Color panel ............................................................................F6
Show/Hide Layers panel ...........................................................................F7
Show/Hide Info panel ...............................................................................F8
Show/Hide Actions panel...................................................................Option-F9
Open Adobe Bridge................................................................... ⌘-Option-O

## OTHER SHORTCUTS

Switch between open documents ..................................................... ⌘-~
Undo or Redo operations beyond last one ................ ⌘-Option-Z/⌘-Shift-Z
Apply Last Filter ......................................................................... ⌘-F
Opens Last Filter Dialog Box......................................................... ⌘-Option-F
Hand Tool ................................................................................. Spacebar
Reset Dialog Box................. Hold Option, Cancel turns into Reset Button, Click it
Increase/Decrease value (in any option field) by 1 unit................Up/Down Arrow
Increase/Decrease value (in any option field) by 10 units.....Shift-Up/Down Arrow
Repeat Last Transformation ...............................................⌘-Shift-T
Measure Angle between Lines (Protractor Function)
........................ After ruler is drawn, Option-Drag end of line with Ruler Tool
Move Crop Marquee while creating.............................Hold Space while drawing
Snap Guide to Ruler ticks............................................Hold Shift while dragging
Highlight Fields in Options bar (n/a for all tools) ...................................... Return
Don't Snap object edge while moving .......................Hold Control while dragging

# Illustrator CS6

## Useful Keyboard Shortcuts: Mac

nobledesktop.com

## TOOLS

| | | | |
|---|---|---|---|
| V | Selection | E | Free Transform |
| A | Direct Selection | Shift-S | Symbol Sprayer |
| Y | Magic Wand | J | Column Graph |
| Q | Lasso | U | Mesh |
| P | Pen | G | Gradient |
| + | Add Anchor point | I | Eyedropper |
| - | Delete Anchor point | W | Blend |
| Shift-C | Convert Anchor point | K | Live Paint Bucket |
| T | Type | Shift-L | Live Paint Selection |
| \ | Line Segment | Shift-O | Artboard |
| M | Rectangle | Shift-K | Slice |
| L | Ellipse | H | Hand |
| B | Paintbrush | Z | Zoom |
| N | Pencil | X | Toggle between Fill & Stroke |
| Shift-B | Blob Brush | Shift-X | Swap Fill & Stroke |
| Shift-E | Eraser | D | Default Fill & Stroke |
| C | Scissors | | (white fill/black stroke) |
| R | Rotate | < | Fill or Stroke w/Color |
| O | Reflect | > | Fill or Stroke w/Gradient |
| S | Scale | / | Fill or Stroke w/None |
| Shift-R | Warp | F | Cycle through Screen Modes |

Double-click tools to bring up options.
Press CAPS LOCK to change tool pointer to crosshair.
Hold down Shift to constrain movement to 45°, 90°, 135°, or 180°.

## SELECTING AND MOVING

To access Selection or Direction Selection tool (whichever was used last)
at any time ............ ⌘ (Command)
To switch between Selection and Direct Selection tools .......... ⌘-Option-Tab
To cycle through tools behind column tool .......... Option-click tool
To make copy while dragging .......... Option
To add to a selection .......... Shift
Move Selection .......... Any arrow key
Move Selection 10 pts .......... Shift-any arrow key
Lock selected artwork .......... ⌘-2
Lock all deselected artwork .......... ⌘-Option-Shift-2
Unlock all artwork .......... ⌘-Option-2
Hide selected artwork .......... ⌘-3
Hide all deselected artwork .......... ⌘-Option-Shift-3
Show all artwork .......... ⌘-Option-3

## PATH EDITING

Join and Average at same time .......... ⌘-Option-Shift-J
Convert Anchor Point tool from Pen tool .......... Option
Switch between Add Anchor Point and Delete Anchor Point tools .......... Option
Add Anchor Point tool from Scissors tool .......... Option
Move anchor point while drawing with Pen tool .......... Spacebar
Create closed path with Pencil or Paintbrush tool ..........
.......... when finished drawing, hold Option and release mouse
Connect to an open (& selected) path with Pencil .......... ⌘-drag

## PAINTING AND TRANSFORMING

Eyedropper tool from Live Paint Bucket tool .......... Option
Samples intermediate color from gradient, picture, etc. with eyedropper .......... Shift
Sets center point and shows dialog .......... Option-click with Tool
Duplicates and transforms selection .......... Option-drag
Transform pattern without transforming object .......... ~(tilde)-drag
Scale proportionally with Selection tool .......... Shift-drag bounding box
Scale from center with Selection tool .......... Option-drag bounding box
Move mesh point along path with Mesh tool .......... Shift-drag
Add mesh point with Mesh tool without changing color .......... Shift-click
Remove mesh point with Mesh tool .......... Option-click

## SHAPES (WHILE DRAWING)

Draw from center .......... Option
Draw from center with dialog .......... Option-click
Constrain proportion .......... Shift
Constrain orientation of polygons, stars, spirals .......... Shift
Move object while drawing .......... Spacebar
Add/subtract sides, points, spiral segments .......... Up or Down Arrow
Decrease inner radius .......... ⌘
Create Continuous duplicates along mouse movement .......... hold ~ while Dragging

## VIEWING & GUIDES

Get Hand Tool (while NOT editing Type) .......... Spacebar
Get Hand tool (while editing Type) ..........
.......... Hold ⌘, then Space. Then continue holding Space but let go of ⌘
Zoom In Tool .......... ⌘-Spacebar
Zoom Out Tool .......... ⌘-Option-Spacebar
Zoom In to exact size .......... ⌘-Spacebar-drag
Hide/Show all tools and panels .......... Tab
Hide/Show all panels except toolbox .......... Shift-Tab
Switch between horizontal/vertical guide .......... hold Option while dragging out a new guide
Release Guide (turns it into a regular path) .......... ⌘-Shift-double-click

## TYPE

Decrease/Increase type size .......... ⌘-Shift-< or >
Decrease/Increase leading .......... Option arrow up or down
Decrease/Increase kerning/tracking .......... Option arrow left or right
Kerning/tracking x 5 .......... ⌘-Option arrow left or right
Decrease/Increase baseline shift .......... Shift-Option arrow down or up
Baseline shift x 5 .......... ⌘-Option-Shift arrow down or up
Align type left, right, center .......... ⌘-Shift-L, R, C
Justify with last line left aligned .......... ⌘-Shift-J
Justify all line .......... ⌘-Shift-F
Reset horizontal/vertical scale to 100% .......... ⌘-Shift-X
Reset kerning or tracking to 0 .......... ⌘-Option-Q

## PANEL SHORTCUTS/FUNCTION KEYS

Show/Hide Brushes .......... F5
Show/Hide Color .......... F6
Show/Hide Layers .......... F7
Show/Hide Info .......... ⌘-F8
Show/Hide Gradient .......... ⌘-F9
Show/Hide Stroke .......... ⌘-F10
Show/Hide Attributes .......... ⌘-F11
Revert file .......... F12
Show/Hide Graphic Styles .......... Shift-F5
Show/Hide Appearance .......... Shift-F6
Show/Hide Align .......... Shift-F7
Show/Hide Transform .......... Shift-F8
Show/Hide Pathfinder .......... Shift-⌘-F9
Show/Hide Transparency .......... Shift-⌘-F10
Show/Hide Symbols .......... Shift-⌘-F11

## LAYERS PANEL SHORTCUTS

Toggle layer between Preview/Outline mode .......... ⌘-click on eye
Show layer while turning-off all others .......... Option-click on eye
Select all items on layer .......... Option-click layer name
Copy selected item to different layer .......... Option-drag selection square in Layers panel
To create the new layer at the top of list .......... ⌘-click
To create the new layer below selected layer .......... ⌘-Option-click

## COLOR PANEL SHORTCUTS

Saturate/Desaturate current color .......... Shift-drag color slider
Change Color Mode .......... Shift-click color bar
Select compliment of current color .......... ⌘-click color bar

## SWATCHES PANEL SHORTCUTS

Create a swatch as a global color .......... Hold ⌘-Shift while creating
Replace a swatch with another .......... Option-drag new swatch over old

## MISC.

(In any panel) Apply a value, but keep value highlighted in panel .......... Shift-Return
Create New Symbol .......... F8
Swap Colors in a Gradient .......... Option-Drag a color stop onto another

Exceptional computer graphics training

NOBLE DESKTOP LLC, 594 BROADWAY, SUITE 1202, NEW YORK, NY 10012
PHONE: 212-226-4149 COPYRIGHT © 2013 NOBLE DESKTOP